Focus on Fine Arts:

VISUAL ARTS

Don L. Brigham

Frederick B. Tuttle, Jr.
Series Editor

nea PROFESSIONAL LIBRARY
National Education Association
Washington, D.C.

Acknowledgment

The author wishes to thank the following art educators for their assistance in developing this publication: Deborah C. Amylon, art teacher, Willett Elementary School, Attleboro, Massachusetts; Rudolf Arnheim, Professor Emeritus of the Psychology of Art, Harvard University and University of Michigan, Ann Arbor; Jerome Hausman, Art Institute of Chicago, and Urban Gateways Center for Arts in Education, Chicago, and Associate Editor, *Art Education*; Jan Irwin, Director of Continuing Education, Rhode Island School of Design, Providence; Eleanor Lazarus, Curator/Director of Education, DeCordova and Dana Museum and Park, Lincoln, Massachusetts; Jo-Anna J. Moore, University of Southern Maine, Gorham, and Maine Alliance for Arts Education, Portland; Charles A. Qualley, Department of Fine Arts, University of Colorado at Boulder, and President, National Art Education Association, Reston, Virginia; Stephen E. Saunders, art teacher, Hill-Roberts Elementary School, South Attleboro, Massachusetts; and Jean Morman Unsworth, Loyola University of Chicago, and Office of Catholic Education, Archdiocese of Chicago.

Printing History
    First Printing: June 1989

Note

The opinions expressed in this publication should not be construed as representing the policy or position of the National Education Association. Materials published by the NEA Professional Library are intended to be discussion documents for educators who are concerned with specialized interests of the profession.

Library of Congress Cataloging-in-Publication Data

Brigham, Don L.
      Visual arts / Don L. Brigham.
          p.   cm. — (Focus on fine arts)
      Bibliography: p.
      ''A jont publication of the National Education Association [and] National Art Education Association.''
      ISBN 0–8106–0304–7
      1. Art—Study and teaching (Elementary)—United States.   2. Art—study and teaching (Secondary)—United States.   I. Title.
II. Series.
N353.B75   1989
707'.1'273—dc20   89–3264
                                                                                    CIP

CONTENTS

The Author

Don L. Brigham is Supervisor of Visual Arts, K-12, Attleboro Public Schools, Massachusetts.

The Series Editor

Frederick B. Tuttle, Jr., is Assistant Superintendent, Needham Public Schools, Massachusetts. A former university professor and education consultant, Dr. Tuttle is the author of *Composition: A Media Approach, Gifted and Talented Students*, and *How to Prepare Students for Writing Tests*; the editor of *Fine Arts in the Curriculum*; and the coauthor of *Technical and Scientific Writing, Characteristics and Identification of Gifted and Talented Students*, and *Program Design and Development for Gifted and Talented Students*, all published by NEA. He also developed the NEA multimedia program *Educating Gifted and Talented Students*.

The Advisory Panel

Robert A. Lague, Music and Drama Teacher, Andover High School, Massachusetts

Sharon H. Rasor, Assistant Professor of Music, Wright State University, Dayton, Ohio

Earl P. Smith, Professor of Art, Troy State University, Alabama

EDITOR'S PREFACE

American people are today concerned with humanistic and cultural matters to a degree unprecedented in their history. [Far] from reflecting this new concern with humanistic and cultural matters, the schools of the nation have let the humanities and the arts languish. (10)*

THE ARTS ARE BASIC

The position of the performing and visual arts in our educational system has not improved appreciably since Alvin Eurich made this observation in 1969. While few would deny the value of the arts, many continually relegate them to the periphery of curricula in most schools. In 1985 the national Parent Teachers Association found that—

Nearly 70 percent of the 1,164 schools recently surveyed by the Alliance of Independent Colleges of Art have experienced cuts in art teachers, courses or program budgets since 1981. Forty percent of these schools expect even further cuts.

Only about 2 percent of the average school budget is spent on arts programs. . . .

Knowledge and skills in music have decreased by 3.3 percent among 9-year-olds and 2.5 percent among 17-year-olds in the past seven years. (10)

To effect a substantive change we need not only a reaffirmation of the importance of the arts, but also practical descriptions of ways that they can begin to fulfill their roles in the educational process. The National Endowment for the Arts gives direction to this need:

Basic arts education must give students the essence of our civilization, the civilizations which have contributed to ours, and the more distant civilizations which enrich world civilizations as a whole. It must also give students tools for creating, for communicating and understanding others' communications, and for making informal and critical choices. (9, p. 13)

Importance of the Arts

Education in the arts plays a major role in three general areas of

---

*Numbers in parentheses appearing in this Preface refer to the References on page 11.

educational impact: societal, instructional, and individual. "[One] of the major goals of education should be to promote the continuation of culture, transmitting values and concepts of civilization from one generation to the next" (13). Through study of the arts we may acquire a cultural record of our past and present. This understanding is necessary to help put ourselves and our value systems into perspective. The necessity of such a perspective has been acknowledged by William Bennett, former secretary of education:

> All students, then, should know some of these works [of art] for a simple reason: they cannot understand the present if they have no understanding of the past. If we cut them off from our culture's past, we automatically make youth aliens in their own culture. And that makes them ill-equipped to succeed in or even understand the world around them. (3)

While students gain knowledge of events and historical movements that shaped society, they also gain insights into the underlying value systems and beliefs of societies and cultures through the arts. "[Humans] experience and give expression to their most deeply held values, beliefs, and images through the arts, and there can be no adequate form of general education that does not include them" (12).

Instructionally, the arts may provide both creative outlets for students to express themselves as well as alternative avenues through which students may understand others' feelings and ideas. Some teachers base their interpretations of a student's learnings primarily on performance on "objective" tests, written essays, or class participation. However, many students who do not perform well through these means are able to show that they understand a concept when encouraged to respond through other means such as art, photography, drama, and dance (14). Ultimately, students must learn how to communicate effectively through tests and essays if they are to succeed in our educational system. But some students must first acquire confidence in themselves. Once they are able to demonstrate that they do understand the concepts, these students often transfer this confidence to responses through other, more "academic," means. Indeed, once a student shows understanding of a concept, the instructional task changes. Instead of stressing the concept itself, the teacher may then focus on the mode of expression.

Moreover, some students learn particular concepts more effectively through the arts than through textbooks and lectures. While developing a program using films and pictures to teach poetry, for example, I found that many students for whom the poems were considered too difficult could accurately state the themes of the poems when they were presented visually in films. I concluded that "once the students have found they can read visual images accompanying a poem, they can [often] read and react critically to the poem itself [in its printed version]" (15). Robert Spillane, Superintendent of Fairfax County (Virginia) Public Schools, summarizes the importance of the arts to all education:

> In any case, an education and a life that ignore vast areas of expression, communication, conceptualization, and innovation—the visual and aural areas—will surely hamstring our future communicators, conceptualizers, and innovators.... Thus, education must give space—albeit in a crowded curriculum—to the arts, which connect thinking and feeling in the aural and visual worlds. (12).

The inability of students and teachers to draw connections among disciplines has resulted in a fragmentation of learning. As students progress from one grade level to the next, this isolation of studies increases. Ernest Boyer, President of the Carnegie Foundation for the Advancement of Teaching, comments on the role arts education may play in overcoming this departmentalization of learning:

> After visiting colleges and schools, I am convinced that students at all levels need to see connections. And I believe that finding patterns across separate disciplines can be accomplished through the arts.... I'm suggesting that the arts give us a language that cuts across the disciplines, help us to see connections and bring a more coherent meaning to our world. (4)

Perhaps the greatest benefit of arts education is to the student as an individual. The "arts can provide the means for communicating thoughts, emotions, and ideas that cannot otherwise be expressed. The arts also contribute significantly to each individual's search for identity, self-realization, and personal confidence" (12). One of the outcomes of the "visual literacy" movement in the 1970s was the introduction of filmmaking as part of many curricula. Students who had previously considered dropping out of school began to use film to share their ideas and feelings with teachers and classmates. They became recognized and valued in the academic envi-

7

ronment because they could interact effectively with others. For the first time they encountered success instead of failure in school. Boyer places this role of the arts at the top of his list: "First, the arts are needed in the nation's schools because they help children express feelings and ideas words cannot convey" (4).

For those students who have particular aptitude in the arts, the inclusion of the arts in education is especially vital. As Elliot Eisner, Professor of Art and Education at Stanford University, observes,

> The inclusion of the arts in the school's curriculum provides opportunity not only for all students to learn to read the arts, but especially for those students whose aptitudes are in the arts. . . . It is hard to discover what one doesn't have an opportunity to practice. Educational equity is an empty ideal when a substantial portion of our children are excluded from the very areas in which their talents reside. (6)

Although the importance of the arts in education has been generally acknowledged for these and other reasons, in most schools the arts are still treated as "frill" areas of the curriculum with the basic instruction focusing on language, mathematics, science, and social studies. When a budget crisis strikes, as it did in California with Proposition 13 and in Massachusetts with Proposition 2 1/2, arts education usually suffers through severe budget cuts or even elimination. Eisner offers several reasons for the marginal position of arts in the curriculum. Among these are views that (1) the arts are emotional, not cognitive; (2) lack of assessment in the arts; (3) the arts are solely creative experiences; and (4) the arts are innate rather then learned (6). To place education in the arts closer to the center of the curriculum, we must address these views and realistically demonstrate vital roles the arts may play within academic curricula. As Bennett states, "Those of us engaged in education must promote the truth that study of the arts increases both our individual capacities for creativity and love for the highest creative work of others" (2).

Underlying Assumptions for the Fine Arts Series

The basic premise for developing this series of monographs on the arts in the classroom is that to accomplish the preservation and transmission of knowledge, skill, values, and culture from generation to generation, we must address the study of the humanities, including the study of visual and performing arts. Four assumptions underlie this premise:

1. All students should have both exposure to and instruction in visual and performing arts throughout elementary and secondary education.
2. Curricula in the visual and performing arts should be presented both as unique disciplines in themselves as well as integral components of other disciplines where appropriate.
3. As with any discipline, visual and performing arts curricula should follow a sequential, organized pattern from kindergarten through grade 12.
4. Finally, the effectiveness of programs and student achievement in visual and performing arts should be assessed based on the program and content of the curricula.

Instruction should not be limited only to those students who display particular talents in the arts. As the National PTA states: "Art is basic to life. It helps us understand ourselves and others. It provides comfort and pleasure through books, music, film, painting and the performing and decorative arts" (10). All students should have the opportunity to enjoy and learn from the arts. Exposure alone is not sufficient, however. "Appreciating a work of art demands intelligent application of perceptual and cognitive resources" (11). Such learning calls for direct instruction.

This instruction should be developmental and sequential from elementary through secondary school, with each year building upon learnings of a previous year. Describing the Discipline-Based Art Education program, Eisner states:

> If a sound art education program were implemented effectively in schools from kindergarten through twelfth grade, youngsters finishing school would be more artistically literate.... Youngsters finishing schooling would understand something about the relationships between culture and the content and form of art. (5)

Too often many educators treat art education as either a separate study isolated from other disciplines or only in relation to other disciplines. Both approaches are necessary for students to learn the content of visual and performing arts as well as the integral relationships between the arts and other disciplines. While the visual and performing arts are disciplines in themselves with their own

9

contents, they are also integral to many other disciplines. When studied in support of other disciplines, however, the arts tend to be viewed only as illustrations of concepts in the more "academic" studies, with little attention being paid to their own content. Consequently, education in the arts should be approached in both ways: as separate disciplines and in relation to other disciplines.

Unless the effectiveness of arts programs is legitimately assessed, work in those curricula will not be highly valued. As Eisner observes, "What we test is what we teach" (6). Consequently, program evaluation should assess the validity of the content, the effectiveness of instruction and, especially, student achievement. Since most student achievement in the visual and performing arts does not lend itself to traditional evaluation procedures, many arts educators base their evaluation on effort rather than actual achievement. As with other disciplines, however, students should be held to appropriate standards and expectations related directly to the instruction and content. In Project Zero, for example, which emphasizes student production, the assessment procedures focus on projects, portfolios, and interviews concentrating on the students' creative processes (8, 15). In the Discipline-Based Arts Education program, "Evaluation of outcomes pertains not only to the products of the students' efforts—the skills, the newfound appreciations, the fresh understandings, the refined judgment that students achieve—but also to the way in which students are engaged in the process of learning" (6). Each program should design its own assessment procedure based on the content of the discipline and the goals of the instructional approach. In the report *Toward Civilization,* the National Endowment for the Arts stresses the importance of assessment in the arts: "Without testing and evaluation, there is no way to measure individual and program progress, program objectives will lack specificity, the arts courses will continue to be considered extracurricular and unimportant" (9, p. 27).

—Frederick B. Tuttle, Jr.
Series Editor

REFERENCES

1. "Arts Education: A Position Statement and Proposed Action." Boston: Board of Education, Commonwealth of Massachusetts, 1975.

2. Bennett, William J. "The Flap." Speech given at National Association of Schools of Music National Convention, Colorado Springs, Colorado, November 24, 1986.

3. _____."Why the Arts Are Essential." *Educational Leadership* 45, no. 4, January 1988.

4. Boyer, Ernest L. *"The Arts, Language and the Schools."* *Basic Education* 2, no. 4, Summer 1987.

5. Eisner, Elliot. "On Discipline-Based Art Education: A Conversation with Elliot Eisner." *Educational Leadership* 45, no. 4, January 1988.

6. _____. *The Role of Discipline-Based Art Education in America's Schools.* Los Angeles: Getty Center for Education in the Arts, 1986.

7. _____. "Why Arts Are Basic." *Basic Education* 31, no. 9, May 1987.

8. Gardner, Howard. "On Assessment in the Arts: A Conversation with Howard Gardner." *Educational Leadership* 45, no. 4, January 1988.

9. National Endowment for the Arts. *Toward Civilization: A Report on Arts Education.* Washington, D.C.: U.S. Government Printing Office, May 1988.

10. National Parent Teachers Association. *Children and the Arts: What Your PTA Can Do.* Chicago: the Association, 1985.

11. Perkins, D. N. "Art as an Occasion of Intelligence." *Educational Leadership* 45, no. 4, January 1988.

12. Spillane, Robert R. "Arts Education Is Not a Frill." Updating School Board Policies. Alexandria, Va.: National School Boards Association, 1987.

13. Tuttle, Frederick B., Jr. ed. *Fine Arts in the Curriculum.* Washington, D.C.: National Education Association, 1985.

14. _____. "Robert's Problem . . . or Ours?—Visuals in the Classroom." *Connecticut English Journal,* Fall 1978.

15. _____. "Visualizing Poetry." *Media and Methods,* May 1970.

16. Wise, Joseph. "Music as a Catalyst for Inter-Disciplinary Education: Attitudes of School Administrators." *ERS Spectrum* 5, no. 2, Spring 1987.

17. Wolf, Dennie Palmer. "Opening Up Assessment." *Educational Leadership* 45, no. 4, January 1988

INTRODUCTION

PROPOSALS FOR REFORMING ART EDUCATION

Powerful political and economic pressures upon the contemporary field of visual art education would reform school art programs in the direction of academic and humanistic scholarship. The well-financed Getty Center for Education in the Arts (G.C.E.A.), through its Institute for Educators, would transform school art into "a subject with content that can be taught and learned in ways that resemble how other subjects are taught in schools" (13, p. 131)*. Former Secretary of Education William Bennett would "train our young people to know, love, and respond to the ... great works of art" that "form an incomparable record of our past" (3, p. 5). This view is affirmed in *Toward Civilization*, a recent publication for the National Endowment for the Arts (N.E.A.), which asserts that "the first purpose of arts education is to give our young people a sense of civilization.... The great works of art ... provide the guideposts. ..." (43, p. 3).

Supporting this orientation, educational policy theorist Ralph Smith "would view art as one of the humanities offered as a part of a curriculum of liberal or general education" (55, p. 4). In philosophical accord with Bennett and the authors of *Toward Civilization*, Smith asserts that "the principal goal of teaching art is the development of the disposition to interpret artworks properly and to appreciate artistic excellence." Students need, he claims, "*an art-historical framework*" (Smith's emphasis) and "an emphasis on the ... classic, masterpiece, or touchstone" (p. 4). Smith believes that these qualities "of excellence in art" (p. 3) can be communicated purely through "conceptual learning" without "creative and performing activities" (p. 5).

The Intended Rescue of Art Education

These politically and economically influential reform projects and proposals are intended to rescue school art education from its putative poor quality and low, ineffectual status throughout the

---

*Numbers in parentheses appearing in the text refer to the Bibliography beginning on page 78.

United States. In a widely distributed promotional booklet, *Beyond Creating* (29), spokespersons for the G.C.E.A. and its Institute for Educators promise "to effect lasting change in the content and quality of visual arts education in America's schools" (29, Foreword) because, purportedly, art education "is accorded such low status" (p. iv) and languishes "on the educational sidelines" (p. 3).

The scholars and educators who prepared the N.E.A. report, *Toward Civilization*, assert that "the arts [in American public schools] are in triple jeopardy: they are not viewed as serious; knowledge...is not viewed as a prime...objective; and those who determine school curricula do not agree on what arts education is" (43, p. 3). Thus, these critics and reformers conclude, arts courses, when they exist at all in schools, are "considered extracurricular and unimportant" (p. 4) and are not "a basic and sequential part of the [total school] curriculum."

Misconceptions

It is evident that these reform efforts are well intended. I perceive no problem with the worthy intention of transforming elementary and secondary art education into a basic subject that is taken seriously by teachers, students, administrators, policymakers and parents. However, I do perceive a problem with the transformed *contents* and *methods* that these powerful agents and agencies of educational reform are proposing for new national programs of school art. Based upon readings of much of their literature, listenings at their seminars, and experience as a curriculum consultant for a G.C.E.A. state planning grant, I am convinced that, though they think otherwise, these well-intentioned reformers *would transform art into something that it is not*. Ironically then, if my perceptions are correct, these reformers and agencies of reform would unintentionally reduce or eliminate *the essential quality of art* while attempting to vivify, strengthen, and extend it in our schools. They would unwittingly, throw out the "baby" (i.e., the necessary and sufficient quality of art) with the "bathwater" of art education's reputed low stature, insignificance, and confusion of purpose in American public schooling. Unless corrected, the reform efforts may succeed in "strengthening" the position of "art" in the schools *by eliminating it* in favor of something that lacks its essential quality and nature.

13

A QUALITATIVE BASIS
FOR REFORMING ART EDUCATION

I am persuaded, by several decades of practical and theoretical experience in the visual arts, that in its essential nature art is a process of shaping experiential qualities (e.g., lines, textures, tonalities, masses, hues, rhythmic patterns) into human meanings and values. It is a distinctly nonverbal and nonmathematical mode both of comprehension and of communication. It is a lively participation and interaction between *the qualities of a human mind* (the whole person that simultaneously perceives and makes art) and *the qualities of human surroundings and objects of interest.*

"Art" is both the interactive process and its outcome—a new, personal "understanding," "interpretation," "meaning," and "value" that is shaped qualitatively both within mind and in art media. The qualitative meaning and value in mind is termed "an image" and its expressive media-form is generally termed "a painting," "a sculpture," or other category of art object.

Both the image-in-mind and the image-in-media are forms of knowledge and vehicles for communication that have cultural and educational significance. Groups of people, such as students and teachers, who are well versed in the qualitative processes and expressive forms of visual art can share humanistic meanings and values that are not available either in verbal language or mathematical quantification and logic.

The purpose of this monograph is to articulate as clearly as possible the essential nature of art, as briefly characterized above, and to describe ways and means of effectively implementing that essential nature in elementary and secondary schools. The ways and means described will not be opposed to the strong contemporary impetus toward educational communication of "our cultural legacy." Rather, since humanistic meanings and values are embedded in the sensuous forms of visual art objects, the proposed "qualitative" contents and methods of visual art education will help all students "read" that legacy *through sense-perceptual interaction with exemplary art objects* that represent the many world cultures that have contributed to the evolution of American civilization.

An underlying premise is that *all* students are potentially capable of experiencing and utilizing the fundamental qualitativeness of art; therefore, it is realistic to propose "qualitative visual art education" for all students at all grade levels.

Chapter 1

WHAT IS QUALITATIVE ART EDUCATION?

ART EDUCATION AND CULTURAL HERITAGES

In 1983, the National Commission on Excellence in Education published a scathing criticism of the state of American public school education. Warning that "our once unchallenged pre-eminence in commerce, industry, science, and technological innovation is being overtaken by competitors throughout the world" (42), the authors of *A Nation At Risk* urged reform of elementary and secondary education "if only to keep and improve on the slim competitive edge we still retain in world markets." Their proposed remedy was to reduce elective curricular offerings and focus upon a core of "Five New Basics"—English, mathematics, science, social studies, and computer science. American arts educators took some heart from the commission recommendation to combine education in these basics with work in the fine and performing arts and foreign languages. Such a combination, according to the commission, constitutes "the mind and spirit of our culture."

Since publication of *A Nation at Risk,* many calls for art education have focused upon "the mind and spirit of our culture." In 1984 Elliott Eisner wrote that "the fundamental human questions are ineluctably enduring and that over the course of human history some extraordinary human beings have made some remarkable efforts to answer these questions" (21, p. 116). Among these are "great humanistic works" in visual art forms that "have as much to say about man and his world as any writer can convey or any historian can describe" (p. 117). These achievements are "there to enhance the lives of those who can 'read' them" (p. 119).

According to Eisner, all students should have access to these artistically expressed cultural meanings and values, and the school "is the primary public institution that can make such access possible for the vast majority of students in our nation" (22, p. 64).

Many education critics and reformers have reinforced the notion that "the mind and spirit of our culture" ought to be communicated to a majority of students through arts education. During his term as president of the National Art Education Association, Edmund B. Feldman wrote that "the desire to preserve civilization, to renew the best of the past . . . needs to be firmly established in every generation. And that is the real job of art education" (26, p. 9). During the same period, Frank Hodsoll, Chair of the National Endowment for the Arts, noted that "the arts express, document, interpret, illuminate, and celebrate human experience and are essential to the vitality and memory of all civilizations" (34, p. 5).

In his report on the status of secondary education in America, former U.S. Education Commissioner Ernest L. Boyer complained that "American young people remain shockingly ignorant about our own heritage and about the heritage of other nations" (5). Noting that the arts are "the means by which a civilization can be measured," he recommended "that all students study the arts to discover how human beings use nonverbal symbols and communicate . . . through music, dance, and the visual arts." This recommendation is reinforced in John Goodlad's national study, *A Place Called School,* which urged reforms that might develop in all elementary and secondary students "an awareness and understanding of one's cultural heritage," including aptitudes for applying "the basic principles and concepts of fine arts and humanities to the appreciation of the aesthetic contributions of other cultures" (30).

Former Secretary of Education Bennett asserted that "one of the primary tasks of our schools" is to "call Americans back to our cultural legacy" (3). He is "cheered" by what he claims is a "fact" that "everywhere about us in recent years we have seen a yearning" for "reaffirmation" of a "cultural and educational restoration" (p. 4). Bennett believes there is a widespread national desire and movement toward the education of all youth in "what is lastingly beautiful in their cultural heritage." Affirming this educational reorientation Frank Hodsoll, chairman of the National Endowment for the Arts, speaks of awakening "the sleeping giant of culture" (35). "The essence" of a new priority for the National Endowment, according to Hodsoll, "comes down to students developing a sense of [not only] how to do the arts, [but] of how to read and interpret the arts, and how to recognize and understand the artistic achievements and expressions of civilization" (p. 103).

Ralph Smith of the Department of Educational Policy Studies at the University of Illinois commends the new "predominantly educational'' commitment and role of the National Endowment (55). With American cultural policy critic Samuel Lipman, he recommends that the Endowment concern itself primarily ''with communicating to our citizens the particular kind of knowledge about ourselves, our world, and most especially the civilized heritage that art enshrines'' (p. 2, citing Lipman [40, p. 14]). Thus, Smith recommends, art education ''can be accommodated to the purposes of traditional liberal education, to humanistic education in the best sense of the term'' (p. 3).

J. Carter Brown, director of the National Gallery of Art, has joined the many reformers who would refocus school art upon ''our common heritage'' (10). Characterizing art museum masterpieces as ''historical documents,'' he proposes that ''it is only through studying such visual documents that new generations can grasp the continuity of their great cultural heritage, which can so enrich their lives.'' Brown bases his recommendations upon findings made as a member of a commission mandated by Congress to inquire into appropriate directions and priorities for the National Endowment for the Arts. Commission members, in their report *Toward Civilization,* unanimously agreed that—

> The first purpose of arts education is to give our young people a sense of civilization. . . . Arts education must give students the essence of our civilization, the civilizations which have contributed to ours, and the more distant civilizations which enrich world civilization as a whole. . . . Very importantly, arts education is essential for *all* students, not just the gifted and talented. (43, p. 3)

However, the panelists reported, basic arts education in our civilization is not now being delivered to the vast majority of students. Unfortunately, ''the artistic heritage that is ours, and the opportunities to contribute significantly to its evolution [are] being lost to our young people'' (p. 4).

VISUAL ART COMMUNICATION

All of these critics of American schooling are in general agreement that a vast and rich store of inherited cultural meanings and values is contained in the forms of art objects and productions, and that this artistically expressed store of meanings and values ought to be made accessible to all students through universal education. But, many of the same critics agree, artistically expressed

17

meanings—especially those of the visual arts—are not accessible through ordinary language. For example, the subtle meanings and values of fine paintings are communicated through sensuous structures of painterly texture, brushstroke, color, tone, shape, edge, and spatial relationship. To communicate such distinctively articulated cultural meanings and values, appropriate sensory-perceptual methods of interpretation and expression must be developed in young people. Such a development is a difficult and complex task. New curricula and teaching methods must be devised, based upon valid insight into the unusual nature of artistic communication. What follows is an effort to clarify that nature.

Insights into Artistic Communication

Speaking and writing for the Getty Center for Education in the Arts (G.C.E.A.), Carnegie Foundation President and former Education Commissioner Boyer urges universal school art education in "human experience that could not be captured by . . . words" (6). According to Boyer, our heritage of visual art objects presents "the most intimate, most profoundly moving universal experiences" through "a more subtle, more sensitive set of symbols" than are available through the verbal or mathematical language systems that prevail in schooling. To be "truly human," everyone "must be able to respond to the subtle messages only the arts convey" (p. 8). Thus, Boyer recognizes and respects the distinctively nonverbal language of artistic conceptualization and communication.

Eisner also recognizes the uniqueness of artistic conception, interpretation, and expression when he states that "the arts present to the competent eye those forms of feeling and insight that only artistic form can reveal" (22, p. 65). "Artistic tasks," he continues, are the kinds of activities that can develop "a range of meanings that exceed [and, thus, must surely be different from] what we are able to say in words" (p. 69). Later he writes that "the arts are testimony that humans have a need to convey and to represent *what cannot be expressed in other forms of representation* [emphasis added]. . . . If "words could say what the visual arts can convey, the visual arts would hardly be necessary" (23, p. 9). Still later, he states that "some meanings are better expressed in visual images. . . . Artistic literacy is the means we use to experience the meanings that . . . artists make possible" (24, pp. 20-21).

In effect, Eisner is arguing that since word systems of conception

18

and communication were found inappropriate and inadequate for articulating profound cultural meanings experienced by exemplary artists, then word systems will also be found inadequate for transmitting the artistic heritage to students. Some other means of educational communication must be employed.

Qualitative Ways of Conceiving and Communicating

Eisner and others have pointed to qualitative ways of acquiring meanings and values in art experience without recourse to conventional verbal analyzing, labeling, describing, explaining, or evaluating. Meanings and values can be "had" directly in the sensuous media of art-making and art-perceiving. This "having" is a constructive, perceptual, and imaginative activity on the part of the person having the art idea, meaning, and value.

In an earlier essay, Eisner writes of the imaginatively constructive way of thinking, knowing, and valuing that is especially evident when students paint:

> To have ideas is, in a sense, to engage in a forming process in which conceptions are abstracted or created; that is, they are formed realizations... children use the images they create as symbols for the world.... This activity is due to their need to construct a knowable world and...convey what they know to others.... [Having and expressing an idea is] what Langer calls a 'symbolic transformation'... (18)

Such processes of qualitative ideation surely are "the particular kinds of mental processes that work in the arts elicits and develops" alluded to by Eisner in *Beyond Creating* (22, p. 66). Elsewhere, Eisner contends that

> The creation of meaning is a biologically determined need of the human organism.... Our conceptions...are not only linguistic, they are visual, gustatory, kinesthetic, and even more.... Meaning is constructed by forming [sensory] patterns that eventually become codes.... Creating meaning requires the ability to use the coding system [i.e., sensory patterning] in a way that will disclose what it is the expressive form contains or implies. (19, pp. 14-15)

Thus, Eisner recognizes and asserts *the primacy of constructive* (i.e., *creative*) *functioning in art* (cf. "the process of imaginative transformation" [23, p. 4]). This recognition does not square with Eisner's enthusiastic support of the G.C.E.A.'s "discipline-based

19

art education" (dbae) project, however. *Beyond Creating* (29) belittles and mocks creativity in art education.*

Harry Broudy, another prominent apologist for the G.C.E.A.'s dbae project, emphasizes "the peculiar powers of the imagination—the image-making function of the mind" (9, p. 14). This constructive power applies equally to processes of "aesthetic perception" (p. 7). According to this view, no object of aesthetic experience is apprehended, interpreted meaningfully, appreciated, and stored in memory for future aesthetic experience *unless it is creatively shaped-in-mind by the perceiving and appreciating person*. Imaginative creativity seems to be the essence of art. It occurs no less in acts of aesthetic perception than in acts of drawing, painting, or sculpturing.

Characteristics of Qualitative Intelligence

Elsewhere Eisner asserts the primacy in all categories of visual art experience of what he (following Dewey) terms "qualitative intelligence." Using Dewey's theories as a basis for his argument, Eisner emphasizes that a qualitative view of intelligence requires a shift from conventional views of mind or intelligence as a fixed quantity of "gray matter" that is preordained to deliver a predictable amount of intellectual service to its carrier. Citing Dewey, he characterizes intelligence as "a verb, a type of action, not a noun, not a quantity of something...possessed" (17, p. 113).

Educational philosopher Maxine Greene agrees with Eisner and Dewey that intelligence, or mind, is a dynamic process that shapes and enhances its own form, content, and potentiality through experiential encounters with the world (32, p. 24). These theorists agree that mind is a complex and dynamic structure of energies that reaches out through all the senses to its pulsating environment. Through selective assimilation of perceivable qualities, *the mind reorganizes itself*: it accommodates its dynamic structure to the received sensory impressions, and thus it generates a new, multisensory structure of intelligence and knowledge. The new struc-

---

*According to dbae educators Clark, Day, and Greer, in dbae theory and practice, "Art is viewed as a subject with content that can be taught and learned in ways that resemble how other subjects are taught in schools" (13, p. 131). They clarify their confidence in noncreatively literal and denotational approaches as follows: "DBAE is a developed understanding of the visual arts for all students . . . similar to understandings that educators expect from formal study of such subjects as science, mathematics, or political science" (p. 138).

ture is a sensuously articulated "conception," "idea," "symbolic form," and "meaning." Any artistic conception, meaning, and value is a self-generated *reconstruction* of preexisting sensory structures of a human mind. Thus understood, "mind" is a dynamic organism that is always renewing itself.

From Dewey's perspective, acquired meanings and values build up the mind. His special term for a built-up mind, at every stage of its development, is "formed disposition" (16, p. 266). At any point in the developing life of a person, that person's "formed disposition" is predisposed to enter anew into the stream of experience and, thus inevitably, to alter and renew its "disposition":

> Consciousness is always in rapid change, for its marks the place where the formed disposition and the immediate situation touch and interact. It is the continuous readjustment of self and world in experience . . . the more acute and intense in the degree of the readjustments that are demanded. . . . Its animus is toward further interactions. (16, pp. 266, 264)

It wants to express its liveness, and life is constant evolution and change. Hence there is continuous cognitive and affective change: "The *work* of art remakes the maker" (17, p. 282). All artistic experiences, ideas, understandings, memories, and products, including the cognitive processes of attention and perception, analysis and synthesis, comparison and contrast, transformation, and creative expression in art media, are "mind-altering" (23, p. 2).

Qualifying Powers of Artistic Intelligence

Philosopher John Randall, Jr. defines artistic processes as "powers of qualification" (47, p. 276). For example,

> [T]he particular color of a surface is . . . not "immediately given," but is "mediated" by a long experience, certainly, and probably also by reflection or thought—by what may even be called "inquiry.". . . Such a simple quality . . . is the outcome of . . . processes of "qualification." (47, pp. 278–79)

For Randall, the power of a painter, a poet, or any sensitive and intelligent percipient of painting or poetry, is a lively capacity for "cooperation" between previously developed qualities of mind and qualities encountered in the dynamic world. A painter who perceives and depicts a subtle, unusual quality of green grass thus reveals "unsuspected 'qualities' in grass." This "power" accounts for "the enormous fertility of painting or poetry in revealing new

21

visual, new perceptual powers in things—in 'enhancing the significance,' as we say, of the visible world'' (47, pp. 281–82). It can vivify what we have ''encountered before but . . . not seen'' (17, p. 12).

For Greene, as for Randall and Eisner, ''Art is the transfiguration of the commonplace'' (33, p. 129). Aesthetic intelligence brings ''what Virginia Woolf called a 'shock of awareness,' and experience that shakes conventional certainties . . .'' (p. 132). ''This is what can happen,'' writes Green (pp. 125-26), ''when a person is empowered to be present to a Cezanne landscape or a Beethoven quartet or a Bergman film or a Wallace Stevens poem. . . . All depends on the degree to which energies are moving out. . . , on the quality and intensity of involvement, on breaking of habitual frames.'' Such empowerment of student minds is a fundamental purpose of qualitative visual art education.

Artistic Knowledge

The knowledge that is formed through Randall's ''powers of qualification'' is not denotational and propositional—not present in consciousness as a linguistic system of word names, descriptions, and explanations—but rather is sensuous and configurational. It is a mental composition of experienced sensory-concrete qualities, commonly termed ''a mental picture.'' This artistic cognition is a symbolic representation of some category of experience. Until modified by future experience, it stands in mind as the embodiment of that particular realm of human knowledge. Each embodiment is properly termed *an image*. Because it grew out of personal experience, it is loaded with feeling.

As Harry Broudy asserts,

From the day of birth the mind is being stocked with images. . . . It is this imagic-conceptual store that is activated whenever we read or speak or listen to speech. We comprehend *with* these resources. . . . [Arts] education enriches the store of images that makes comprehension of concepts possible and comprehensive. (pp. 347–50)

Broudy thus recognizes the educationally significant role that visual artistic ''powers of qualification'' can play in comprehensive schooling. Arts experiences can generate a store of personal images from which more abstract forms and systems of knowledge are generated. Thus, visual artistic powers are educational fundamentals.

In his ''pedagogic creed'' of 1897, John Dewey explained the

22

educationally fundamental nature of activities that build up an imaginative base of knowledge:

> What a child gets out of any subject is simply the images which he himself forms with regard to it. . . . Much of the time and attention now given to the preparation and presentation of lessons might be more wisely and profitably expended in training the child's power of imagery and in seeing to it that he was continually forming definite, vivid, and growing images of the various subjects with which he comes in contact in his experience. (14, pp. 148–49)

Qualitative visual art education is an excellent method of "training the child's power of imagery" for improved performance in all subject areas.

Basic Competencies of Qualitative Intelligence

Particular attributes of qualitative intelligence are needed to form meaningful images of Dewey's "various subjects" with which elementary and secondary students come "in contact." According to psychologist and art commentator Rudolf Arnheim, a fundamental competency of qualitative intelligence is the ability to perceive salient features of an object. Seeing intelligently "means grasping some outstanding features of objects—the blueness of the sky, the curve of the swan's neck, the rectangularity of the book, the sheen of a piece of metal, the straightness of the cigarette" (2, p. 43). The significant quality of the whole must be sensed before specific distinctions can be put into proper perspective. The "overall structural features are the primary data of perception, so that triangularity is not a late product of intellectual abstraction, but a direct and more elementary experience than . . . individual detail. The young child sees 'doggishness' before he is able to distinguish one dog from another" (p. 45).

Rudolf Arnheim teaches that we experience the objective world through a developmental progression from perception and assimilation of prominent features to refined discrimination of details, nuances, and subtleties. He insists that "pictorial form grows organically according to definite rules, from simplest to . . . more complex patterns, in a process of gradual differentiation" (p. 171). "Perceiving and conceiving proceed from the general to the specific" (p. 181) though the degree of subtlety and specificity is limited by the degree of interest and/or need on the part of the perceiver: *"any shape will remain as undifferentiated as the [per-*

ceiver's] conception of his goal object permits" (emphasis by Arnheim). For example, on an excursion to Washington, D.C., a group of junior high students encountered Daniel Chester French's sculpture of Lincoln in the Memorial, and Auguste Rodin's bronze *Thinker* at the National Galler of Art. Because of popularized familiarity with the two works, their "goal object" was mere affirmation of popular familiarity. The students hurried on, ignoring the subtleties of form, technique, and detail that might have given them a deeper and more personalized understanding both of the spirit of Lincoln and of profound human introspection.

Art educators are quite familiar with this kind of cursory and undifferentiated perception of visual artistic works. Greene has commented on the phenomenon:

> If, for example, an individual is in a museum along with others, he/she may well move through a room hung with Cezanne paintings and simply take note of which ones are hanging there and of the fact that they were painted by Paul Cezanne. Yes, he/she might recognize an apple here, a pitcher there, the slope of a mountain, the slant of a roof. But that might very likely be all—that and the mild pleasure associated with recognition or response to the richness of color or the space of the gallery itself. (33, p. 124).

Green recognizes what the teacher must do to overcome this superficiality. Students must, somehow, be "released by a teacher to understand the importance of uncoupling from the ordinary when entering the gallery ... to bracket out conventional seeing and expectation for a while" (33). Through imaginative preparation of students, an ingenious teacher can cause them to enter a gallery as though it were a place far removed from everyday convention and routine, yet possessed of subtle distinctions and meanings that each one can discover and relate to personally.

Museum Gallery Tour

Several days before a museum trip, junior high school students were engaged in free associative verbalization activities, seeking and posting words and phrases relating to (1) *serious and solemn* and (2) *fancy and frivolous*. The qualitative synonyms and metaphors that they discovered were displayed on two opposing panels, together with pictures, drawings, and found objects that expressed similar qualities. For instance, next to "austere" was placed a reproduction of Copley's oil portrait of New England puritan-craftsman *Paul Revere* (ca. 1769) and next to *elegant* and *fanciful* were portraits of nobility by mid-eighteenth century French and British masters. The students also displayed dress-up party and school prom pictures under *fancy/frivolous,* and they attached images of formal or religious attire under *serious/solemn.* These associations were extended and elaborated by postings of student designs and color ensembles that matched some of the qualities.

Through such brainstorming and posting qualitative associations with *fancy/frivolous* and *serious/solemn,* each student then chose and wrote ten qualitative expressions in columns under f/f and s/s on eight graph papers. Intervening graph squares of rows that connected opposing adjectives were conceived as scales for evaluating the relative solemnity or frivolity of museum items.

Prepared with the graph papers containing the opposing columns of f/f and s/s expressions, then, each student entered the museum with the assignment of finding two distinctive galleries that seemed to have the overall qualitative flavor of one or the other column of synonymous expressions. When students had chosen their two differing galleries, they selected four items in each gallery. Then they rated each gallery item on all the scales of one graph paper, recording features of fancifulness or sobriety in writing and drawings, in their sketchbooks.

On succeeding school days, the eighth and ninth graders engaged in "debates" (arguing with pictorial collages as well as with words) that supported or denied their gallery choices. Through these "contests," students sharpened their abilities for recognizing distinctive qualities of artistic form, style, and subtlety in a museum gallery.

This example demonstrates a prime competency of artistic intelligence: *qualitative differentiation.* A second essential characteristic of qualitative intelligence, according to Arnheim and others (e.g., Langer [37]), is the grasp of structural dynamics in an art object. According to this view, a fine art object has, in addition to its inventory of sensuous elements, an overall structure of implied force and movement. The implied rhythms, counter-rhythms, inferred directions, and counterdirections of the art object project a perceivable dynamic expression and meaning though the piece is actually still. There is a lively "pattern of forces" (2, p. 453) that articulates expressive meaning; for example, "elation," or "aggression." Friedlander (in Arnheim [2, p. 448]) writes that an aesthetically perceptive person can "find expression even in inanimate objects, such as the columns of a temple." For example,

For a good architect, a column is an animated, suffering, victorious, supporting, and burdened being. The hardly measurable gentle swelling of the contour expresses strength, tension, pressure and resistance. (2, p. 448)

25

Thus, a fine art object can be expressively understood though the perceiver may have little prior experience with the subject matter presented. Expression inheres in the dynamic sensory composition given a subject matter by an artist.

Philosopher Susanne Langer advises us (38, p. 84) that "the form . . . needs to be construed before one can appreciate it." Grasp of "artistic import" requires an imaginative *re-construction* of the dynamic sensory structure that articulates the object's human meaning and value. Such a process is equally required for understanding and appreciating poetry. English professor Gabriele Rico describes this process of poetic interpretation:

> Initially, there is a sweeping apprehension. . . . Such characteristics . . . as motif, recurring image, balance rhythm invite global response . . . a dominant impression . . . scanning movements in which the eye travels over the most compelling features to create a Gestalt . . . the core of subsequent exploration. . . . [S]ynthesis is the result of a dialectic between the initial sense of configuration and the emerging detail . . . undergoing continuous modification. . . . (50, pp. 45–46)

If we follow Rico's process of poetic interpretation (cf. 50, pp. 47–52), we gain insight into appropriate qualitative processes for construing meaning and value in objects of visual art. In accordance with this concept of qualitative analysis and synthesis, the student who attends intelligently to a fine painting, sculpture, print, film, or photograph will first scan the object for its overriding gestalt quality. Having gained an initial, global impression, the arts-educated student will then be able to discover and represent in art media the many levels of qualitative structure that elaborate and reinforce the initial gestalt perception and that ultimately can communicate to him/her the whole meaning of the painting, photograph, or other art object.

Following Langer's and Rico's methodology, a group of seventh graders interpreted a color reproduction of George Caleb Bingham's "Fur Traders Descending the Missouri" (1845, oil on canvas, Metropolitan Museum of Art, New York).

Qualitative Re-Construction of a Painting

Twenty-two girls and boys were arranged in a semicircle facing a color reproduction of Bingham's painting. Students noticed the square shape of the painting, commenting that squarishness is calm and restful. They gradually discovered that the overall quality of restfulness is

26

reinforced by the horizontal shape of the canoe that rides low in the water. They further noted that the boy leans casually at midship, the adult canoeist sits quietly at stern (barely moving the paddle that treads water), and the shadowy animal (tied lightly to the prow) sits erect but calm. These three restful characters seemed to stare calmly out of the canvas toward the seventh graders.

Finding the Overall Pervasive Gestalt. On an easel pad near the repro- duction, the art teacher wrote overall-impression words and phrases proposed by the students. Subsequently, the students decided that the painting is "about" peacefulness, relaxation, and contentment. This was their overall gestalt perception and interpretation.

Evaluating the Initial Gestalt Impression. The teacher asked the stu- dents to examine their initial interpretation of "peacefulness, relaxation, and contentment." All class members looked for and recorded pictorial qualities that seemed to echo the primary perception. Using chalks, colored papers, sponges, charcoal, erasers, cotton, blotters, tempera paints, ink, pens, and brushes, they produced graphic and painterly reports of sensory patterns and figures that seemed to confirm the ini- tial class hypothesis of calmness and peace. Those who rejected the initial gestalt hypothesis depicted visual evidence supportive of their contrary impressions.

Arguing the Case. Evaluative "reporting" was through visual display of all the student findings. The students noticed and then clustered their reports that were conceptually related. It became evident that only half the class reinforced the initial gestalt perception of calmness and peaceful unconcern. Three students attended to the muted and hazy background colors and the peaceful, soft, "flats" (like stage flats) of trees fading to the pastel-tinted, blurred horizon and sky. Two students asserted that the picture is "cheerful" and "lively." They called atten- tion to the "ringing" colors of the canoeist's red blouse and cap-tassel, "blaring" against the brilliant blue of the boy's blouse.

Three students found an "evil," and "threatening" quality in the Bingham painting. Their "evidence" was as follows: the furry, silhouet- ted animal is the darkest quality of the whole composition. Though teth- ered, the mysteriously crouching animal is "the boss," situated near the prow, "leading" the two humans. This "boss" is malevolent. Per- haps a half-wild wolf or fox, it is leading these unsuspecting humans to- ward an unknown fate over tarnished-yellow water. The unknown fate is indicated by the haze that dissolves all horizons. Disturbing indica- tors are the bare, broken, dead branches and stumps that poke up from the water just beyond the canoe. They "point" metaphorically to- ward the unknown future beyond the prow of the canoe. Most threat- ening is a stump in the foreground; it seems to be a skull-like head thrust up and back in agony.

Reinterpreting the Painting. All students and the teacher were fascinat- ed by the "evil" and "threatening" interpretation of the three students. Life metaphors entered into class discussion: Contented humans sometimes "don't know what's in store for them." Ignorance is bliss, but "watch out" for evildoers." "We're all in the same boat," evildoers and good people alike. Life is a mystery (evidenced by the blurred, endless surroundings) and we're all alone, ignorant of the meaning, or "point" (a direction and intent metaphor expressed by the forward-thrusting prow of the canoe and several dead branches) of it all.

A final class consensus was that the painting primarily meant "mystery" and "life alone in the unknown," but a secondary and important message was that a bland, unconcerned and casual lifestyle is "spiced," "tinged," and "sparked" by a "hint" of evil. All in all, the students felt that Bingham's painting is enlivened by the mysterious animal silhouette, at the canoe's prow, that contrasts markedly with the yellowish haze surrounding it. It wonderfully counterbalances the two complacent humans.

Student Gains from Group Study of Painting

The seventh graders acquired many valuable art competencies. They learned how to attend to the *overall expressive form* (gestalt) of an art object rather than merely to its literal content. They discovered how that overall composition communicates *a pervasive quality of meaning*.

With the pervasive quality or general impression in mind, the students learned to examine subordinated compositional elements, details, and subjects (e.g., the smooth, unrippled water, the muted and hazy background, the "ringing" and "blaring" notes of red and blue, the shadowy, silhouetted wolf or fox, the dead stumps that "poke" and "point") for echoes of or contrasts with the overall, pervasive quality. They found that the meaning of an artistic whole is subtle, that sustained and progressive study reveals paradoxical elements and details. These paradoxical elements can give "spark" and "spice" to an artistic whole.

In their search for secondary and tertiary themes of both reinforcement and contradiction, the students demonstrated what English professor Rico terms a "dialectic between initial sense of configuration and emerging detail," and they were able to practice "continuous modification" of an initial interpretation based upon their progressively more acute and subtle discernments of compositional similarities and contrasts. Throughout their process of increasingly subtle discernment, the seventh graders *reflected* back and forth between fine details and the compositional whole. The process included perceiving and reasoning by *metaphor, analogy, synesthesia* (blending sensory modalities), and *empathy* (projecting

28

subjective feelings into objects).

Further, the students learned to *share* and *collaborate*. They found that their learning was enhanced by free and easy give-and-take among peers and with their teachers.

GOALS OF QUALITATIVE EDUCATION

When elementary and secondary students acquire and use abilities for discerning and re-presenting the qualitative meanings of art objects from many world cultures, they are empowered with interpretive skills for finding meaning and value in many things of their immediately surrounding world. They have acquired what Broudy (9, p. 22) terms "an allusionary base" for transfer of their art images—the memory images that they have formed through their encounters with cultural art objects—to new things, events, people, and environments that they want to better understand and absorb into personal value systems.

In a sense, they will have acquired a qualitative lexicon. Henceforth, encountering new experiential "words," they will have qualitative synonyms, analogies, and allusions available to translate the encountered unknowns into imagery that is personally meaningful and full of feeling. The imagery is meaningful both because it is shaped out of personal encounters and initiatives—it is self-made—and because it functions symbolically. A personally fashioned qualitative image henceforth *means* (i.e., is the referential personal symbol for) some category of experience that is known and valued as an integral part of oneself.

Specific Student Achievement Goals

Specific student achievement goals of an approach to visual art education that focuses upon the student's own qualitative interpretation and creative representation of meanings and values latent in the sensuous forms of exemplary cultural art objects may be articulated as follows: The elementary or secondary visual arts student will be able to (1) *perceive* and represent in art media the essential (i.e., the necessary and sufficient) qualitative patterns that infer meaning in exemplary cultural art objects; (2) metaphorically *assimilate* perceived qualitative patterns with personal memory images (including those shaped by personal art-making ventures and

29

by art history studies); (3) *accommodate* the newly conceived qualitative imagery by recalling it to interpret new, qualitatively similar objects, persons, or events; (4) *associate* human feelings and values with qualitative interpretations and memory images; and (5) *apply* both two- and three-dimensional art media to create personally meaningful qualitative imagery.

Art Programs Aimed at Stated Goals

Students who are expected to perceive, assimilate, accommodate, associate, and apply personal experiences to the *qualitative contents* of cultural heritage objects will require many experiences in the specialized, nonverbal "language" of sensory conceptualization and communication. Quality art reproductions, both printed and slide- or film-projected, ought to be readily available in art studio-classrooms. Occasionally, original art objects should be brought into the classroom. Whenever possible, students of all grade levels should travel to places where they can encounter exemplary cultural objects.

Verbal-analytical discussion and evaluation of encountered cultural objects or their reproductions are ancillary rather than primary functions of qualitative art study. Primarily, students are stimulated and guided to perceptually abstract the salient qualitative features from a sensuously expressive cultural art object. As Eisner points out, "It is through the sensory system that the child learns to abstract sensory concepts from the world: the gustatory experience of sweetness is known before the word 'sweet' is affixed to the concept. The process of abstraction within each of the sensory modalities . . . exemplifies the constructive use of cognition" (20, p. 12). Young students' "abstractions" will be both in their heads and in their hands. They will be challenged by their teachers to represent perceived patterns with crayons, markers, paints, clays, and other malleable materials, fabrics, wires, sticks, or stones. As they do so, they will be invited to propose words and phrases that are "like" the patterns represented.

Sometimes the words will be descriptive and literal; more often they will be figuratively or synesthetically expressive (a synesthetic expression is a sensory crossover, such as a mixture of temperature, "hot" [kinesthetic], with color, "red" [visual]). Further, students will be encouraged and helped to make analogical and metaphori-

30

cal connections between the qualities they are detecting and transforming and their personal interests and experiences. These are among the ways that elementary and secondary students can be induced to acquire and use the special qualitative "language" of perception and expression that is the essence of visual arts experience and knowledge.

A class of fifth graders was stimulated and guided to respond to the salient expressive features of Vincent van Gogh's *Starry Night* by an activity of observation and painting with watercolor felt-tip markers. Sometimes the classroom reproduction was turned upside down to deflect attention from its literal subject matter and to focus student perceptions upon the dynamic patterns of brushstrokes and colors that express van Gogh's feelings about his "starry night" experience. (Students turned their large artpapers around in accord with the inverted reproduction.)

Student felt-tip marker studies of van Gogh's expressive form were guided and enhanced by short periods of physical activity when the teacher and a brave and kinesthetically oriented student led the group through rhythmic sequences of gestures emulating movements sensed in the form of *Starry Night*.

Finally, when class members felt that they had "captured" the most important shapes, marks, and directions of movement that "stand out" in van Gogh's work, they engaged in group brainstorming of words, phrases, and analogous experiences such as "whirlpool," "tornado," and "fire" that, they felt, "go with" the qualities of the painting. The brainstorm offerings were written on a large paper and displayed before the students. This led to further discussion of relevant personal experiences.

Students associated the exciting dynamics of *Starry Night* with a basketball game and with a rock music concert. Some students modeled an imagined basketball movement while others captured it with marker strokes and colors. One group modeled a rock performance, while another tried to express the dynamic quality of the event with patterns of color.

During a subsequent visual art class, fifth graders investigated van Gogh's life and the evolution of his painting style by reference to a video presentation. Through discussions following the presentation, they shared perceptions of correspondences between inner human feelings, described and demonstrated in the video documentary, and stylistic features that they identified in *Starry Night* and other van Gogh paintings.

Essential Qualitative Art Abilities

To achieve the goals of qualitative education in the visual arts, students need to acquire and use a number of basic competencies. Given a sequentially organized program of qualitative learning activities, from primary grades through high school, the mature visual arts student may reasonably be expected to be able to—

1. Sustain a focused attention upon expressive qualities of art objects for extensive periods of time. Avoid conventional, stereotypical perception and interpretation (delay closure).
2. Grasp primary overall, dynamic features of art objects. Intuit the figurative and metaphorical rather than literal meanings of overall, gestalt features.
3. Progressively abstract and figuratively or metaphorically interpret the secondary and tertiary qualitative patterns, themes, motifs, and details. Perceive and reflect upon qualitative resonances, "echoes," contrasts, or conflicts with primary overall gestalt impressions.
4. Freely associate the perceived qualitative patterns, themes and motifs of art objects with personal memories. Continue to think metaphorically rather than literally. Sketch and otherwise articulate these personal memory associations.
5. Empathize with perceived art objects, projecting personal feelings and values into their qualitative patterns, themes, and motifs. Express these associated personal feelings and values with visual and tactual as well as verbal media.
6. Interpret qualitative patterns synesthetically (e.g., "hear" "vibrant" colors; use body gesture to express visual rhythms, directional thrusts, and countermovements).
7. Freely improvise; invent variations on perceived qualities. (Sketch and otherwise depict exaggerations, reversals, and other inventive transformations of qualities seen in the object.)
8. Use library and media center research to find art-historical, cross-cultural, and stylistic connections (i.e., analogies) with art object qualities being encountered and interpreted.
9. Make a qualitative report (e.g., a painting, collage, assemblage, or model) that demonstrates one's interpretation of the overall meaning of a qualitatively experienced art object.
10. Originate qualitative forms. Employ all the perceptual and interpretive abilities given in 1–9 above to create personally meaningful qualitative objects in a variety of visual art media.

Chapters 2 and 3 describe appropriate curricular activities for developing these competencies.

Chapter 2

QUALITATIVE VISUAL ART EDUCATION IN THE SCHOOLS

Art educators may plan and conduct a variety of activities to develop essential visual art abilities. These activities should be designed to help students grasp and appreciate the qualitatively formed meanings of inherited cultural art objects. They should also help students express meanings of personal value through their own art productions and apply their art-induced qualitative intelligences and appreciation to a wide range of present-day environmental and social contexts and life experiences.

ELEMENTARY SCHOOL ART EXPERIENCES

At the outset it may be well to state what we ought *not to* expect to see in an elementary school that is devoted to the qualitative artistic development of all students. We ought *not to* expect an itinerant art specialist rushing about from classroom to classroom, hurrying children through 30- to 35-minute activities with minimum supplies and within a sensuously barren "regular classroom" environment. We ought *not to* expect holiday art or school and classroom decorations to be the primary output of art class time. Finally, we ought *not to* expect art student participation in poster contests or any other competitions that distract from primary contents and competency objectives of a qualitative art program.

These three negative characteristics inhibit the development of a qualitative art program for several reasons. First, an itinerant art teacher has neither the time nor the appropriate environmental resources to communicate valuable cultural content through student sensory interactions with examples of visual fine art. Second, holiday and decoration conceptions are generally stereotypic and they often inhibit rather than nourish open, experiential inquiry and innovation. Third, contests inevitably focus students on concepts and criteria of competitive achievement that are extrinsic to the valuable cultural content and qualitative thinking/art-making skills that ought to be the prime learning objectives of excellent present-day visual art education.

33

Ideal Conditions of Qualitative Art Education

In elementary schools committed to the advancement of cultural learning and expression in all students, we may expect to find a full-time, resident, art-certified teacher in each building of approximately 350 students, with additional full- or part-time art specialists to serve larger student populations. Each student in grades 1 through 6 should study art qualitatively for at least 100 minutes weekly. These experiences should occur in specialized art rooms that contain appropriate art tables, easels, sink counters, slide and film projectors, art display surfaces and shelves, and plenty of bins and shelf-counter units for ready student access to hands-on as well as eyes-on materials. Qualitative art teachers need access to a wealth of cultural art resources, including large, good-quality color prints; slides; filmstrips; videotapes; and a library of fine art books representing world cultures, past and present. These visual study resources may be made available through school library and educational media facilities, though, ideally, they are directly available in the specialized art rooms.

Adjustments

When ideal conditions for qualitative education are not available, adjustments and adaptations can be made that will minimally provide for the development of the fundamental interpretive and expressive competencies identified in Chapter 1.

Ordinary classrooms can be used effectively by ingenious and resourceful teachers. If large and prime quality art reproductions cannot be provided, small, inexpensive reproductions may be obtained from many sources and perhaps copied by color xerography for distribution among large numbers of students seated at desks in the regimented row patterns characteristics of old-fashioned classrooms. If through occasional trips to museums and other public display facilities, or short-term loans and displays within school buildings and classrooms, groups of students are introduced to actual cultural heritage objects, they will be able to imagine the real features of the small, low-cost pictorial reproductions.

Using the simplest of graphic and collage-assembly media, students in old-style regimented and aesthetically sparse environments can still be helped to find the expressive forms and personal meanings that are latent in art objects representing many world cultures.

Lesson Procedures

With minimal eyes-on and hands-on media, elementary students were able to interpret and assimilate the qualitative meanings of reproduced art objects using the following procedures.

A group of fourth graders faced large color reproductions of Edvard Munch's three oil paintings, *Anxiety* (1894), *The Scream* (1893), and *Red Virginia Creeper* (1900). Their art teacher stood at an easel to one side and recorded the words and phrases uttered by students to represent their gestalt impressions of the overall qualitative meaning of the three paintings considered as an expressive unit.

Individual class members said that the set of three paintings meant "upset," "scared," "freaked-out," "worried," and "crying for help." Through group discussion and decision making, students selected specific words and phrases that best represented a group hunch of the overall meaning of the three painting. Each student then responded with art media to the teacher's assignment: "Show what you see that is common to the three paintings and that supports the class hunch." Using crayons, chalks, and felt-tip markers on papers of various sizes and colors, each individual quick-sketched his or her abstractions of selected pictorial qualities that "went with" the classwide perception of aloneness, fright, and helplessness seen in Munch's three paintings. A subsequent display and discussion of these quick-sketch abstractions revealed that a majority of fourth graders found expressive significance in (1) the placement of an isolated, greenish-faced person who looks outward beseechingly toward students in a lower quadrant of each painting, (2) the contrast between the deathly green facial hues of the beseeching faces and the backgrounds that feature red-orange skies and "red creeper" vine (the red vine crawls up the walls of a blocky house with blank-white window "eyes" in the middle distance of Munch's 1900 painting), and (3) the nervously curved and twisted shapes and brackish colors of landscapes and figures behind beseeching, screaming children in foregrounds.

Students also sketched and remarked that the bridgelines that slant off to the left in two paintings were harsh, rigidly confining, and "funneling," as though they might suck the beseeching children back into some frightening unknown. Students also drew and expressively interpreted the undulating "dizzying" lines of some pictorial elements that clash dynamically with the rigid diagonals of bridges and the big, blocky shape of the house in the 1900 canvas. The teacher asked that each student reflect upon a personal experience that might be pictorially represented by using one or more of the ways that Munch expressed loneliness, fright, and helplessness in his paintings.

Students were advised that a discussion of time, place, and intention of European Expressionism would occur at the outset of their next class. They were also advised that during their next art periods they would be asked to experimentally produce "Expressionist" paintings or pastels representing their memories of lonely, frightful, and helpless-feeling experiences.

It is notable that in this sample lesson the teacher imposed no predetermined interpretation of Munch's meanings upon the students. A major premise of qualitative art education is that students can and ought to perceive and think for themselves. To preempt their thinking by imposing "authoritative facts" about Expressionism and abut Munch's artistic intentions would block and stunt the creative development of student minds.

In the next sample lesson, third graders practiced imaginative picture-making from verbal clues. They discovered how the verbal clues provoked differing memories from each class member.

Student crayon, marker, tempera, and collage compositions, completed during a prior class, were set before a group of third graders as they listened to a replay of a teacher-made, audiotaped description of a painting by Swiss artist Paul Klee.

Students were asked to listen closely to the replay while viewing a written display of the words they were hearing, and while looking at their earlier work to determine if "anything has been left out of what is described on tape and the display."

To tax their qualitative imaginations, the teacher included in the audiotape a description of a reproduced painting the students *had not yet seen.*

The sky is dark brown but lighted with a checkered shaft of lighter brown that falls on a giant wave near the center of the picture. The falling light makes a checkerboard pattern of light yellow and pale blue squares on the wave and dark blue sea. Three sea creatures leap in the giant wave. They are frightened by a man in a boat who thrusts a red harpoon at the mouth of the high-flying creature. There are two tears of blood. The bleeding creature looks like a giant shrimp but the others are a fish and a seal. They look scared. Their skins have triangles and diamonds and stripes of violet and pink. The top of the rowboat and the man's shirt and shorts also have triangles and diamonds but they are orange and pale yellow. The man stands up, shoving his harpoon with both arms. His red legs are very long and thin. (Adapted from lesson by Stephen E. Saunders, Hill-Roberts Elementary School, South Attleboro, Massachusetts)

The audiotape was replayed while students worked. When all com-

36

positions were finished and tacked up before the class, the teacher displayed the mystery art print, a color reproduction of Klee's *Sinbad the Sailor* (also titled *Battle Scene from the Comic Fantastic Opera* The Seafarer).

As they compared and contrasted their imaginative interpretations of lettered and spoken language with the Klee reproduction, students expressed surprise. They expressed appreciation of the many variations that they, as a class of individuals, had produced. With their teacher, they discussed the basis of the variations. Each student had had different earlier, personal experiences with the verbally described pictorial elements. Each had had a differing memory bank from which to draw relevant pictorial imagery.

Students also indicated that they felt a kinship with the adult artist, Paul Klee; they felt that they shared an understanding and appreciation of the primal and mythic event depicted in *Sinbad the Sailor*. Their teacher asked them to look up Klee in their school resource art library in preparation for their next art period when they would explore Klee's method of improvising pictorial imagery by experimenting freely with multisensory materials.

Through this lesson, students discovered the significance and use of individually differing memory resources for imaginative picture-making. They also discovered personal affinities with the creative imagination of an adult master artist. With an earned sense of affinity with the mind and spirit of a world-famous artist, each student gained confidence and courage for future art endeavors.

The two foregoing sample lessons demonstrate an "inductive" model of teaching and learning. This is a model well articulated by Jerome Bruner (11). Predetermined adult conclusions *are not* dispensed to students but are considered to be the natural and logical *outcomes of inquiry learning activity*. The task of the teacher is to hold adult conceptions (e.g., textbook "facts") in abeyance while inducing students along paths of *encounters with qualities* that are directly relevant to the conceptions and values that are appropriate for their developmental progress through the elementary grades. This organic progress toward *self-generated and self-articulated* knowledge, meaning, and value is entirely consistent with Dewey's conception of the human mind as "animus . . . toward further interactions" (16, p. 264), with Eisner's notions of "the creation of meaning" (19, pp. 14–15), and Langer's advice that "the form needs to be [self-] construed" before "artistic import" can be realized and appreciated (38, p. 84).

Early Elementary Art Experiences

Experienced, art-certified teachers of the public school district with which I have been associated for three decades inform me that they believe that primary-grade students can grasp and use almost any concept or qualitative thinking process if it is appropriately presented. These teachers do not hesitate to present their students with art conceptualizing and interpreting tasks that many adults believe are too difficult. For example, they often present metaphorical reasoning tasks wherein things having differing conventional identity and function are to be synthesized on the basis of qualitative similarity. Psychologists who value human creativity define such competencies as "fluency," "flexibility," and "originality." Philosopher and arts educator Maxine Greene characterizes the competencies as "breaking habitual frames," transfiguring the commonplace, and escaping "the petrified world" (33, p. 134). Three sample lessons follow.

Groups of first and second graders were invited to interpret dadaist, surrealist, and primitivist objects of art metaphorically and empathetically. The primary grade students metaphorically spoke of dadaist Meret Oppenheim's *Fur-covered Cup, Saucer and Spoon* (1936) as a "plate-nest," a "set of animal dishes," and a "feather-dish and hair-cup." They characterized surrealist artist René Magritte's *The Conqueror* as a "dressed-up gravestone," a "wooden man getting married," and a "boardman on the moon dressed to go to an alien restaurant." And they described Max Ernst's surreal *Elephant Celebes* as an "elephant tank," "a metal elephant-bull," and "an elephant tank-robot." Using felt-tip markers and oil-pastel crayons, students created their own compositions based on metaphoric integration of two or more disparate realities. For instance, first graders pictured "a hamburger hat," "a camel slide," "a porcupine toothbrush," and "rubber mud."

To help her primary graders break habitual frames of reference, one art teacher caused her students to react empathetically to Georgia O'Keeffe's enlargements of flowers. First and second graders responded to color reproductions of *Jimson Weed, The White Trumpet Flower* (1932), and *An Orchid* (1941). The huge, white trumpet flower that is surrounded by deep blue, wave-like leaves in the 1932 oil painting was interpreted as "a flower-pool that you could fall into," "a giant funnel you're flying over," and "something that could suck you in and eat you." Students then used various media and techniques to enlarge their own flower studies and to invest the flower forms with extravagant and magical powers. (Lesson by Deborah C. Amylon, Willett Elementary School, Attleboro, Massachusetts)

As an elementary lesson in warm-cool expression, the teacher displayed art examples from various cultures, showing how various subject matters can be treated both realistically and abstractly. (Cf. color reproductions in Chapman [12, pp. 18-21, 40, 106.]) Though their arrangement was scrambled, half the displayed prints were predominantly warm-hued and the other half were cool-hued. The teacher conducted the lesson as follows:

Teacher: "Tell me if the pictures *feel* the same or different. Are some 'happy' and some 'sad'?"

On an easel sheet, below "HAPPY" and "SAD," the teacher lettered student selections. Under "HAPPY," the teacher named the student selections of van Gogh's *Sunflowers* and Monet's *Bassin d'Argenteuil*. Under "SAD," she listed student selections of *Stone Bridge* and Monet's evening scene *Poplars*.

Teacher: "Tell me if some pictures feel 'excited' but others feel 'peaceful and restful'."

Under "EXCITED," the teacher recorded student selections of "the mess of colors, scribbles, and shapes"(Kandinsky's *Painting with Yellow, Improvisation*), and "the flowers" (van Gogh); under "PEACE and REST," "the people in a park" (Seurat's *Sunday Afternoon*), the "trees by a river" (Monet's *Poplars*), and "the one with sailboats" (Monet's *Bassin*).

Teacher: "If you were to think of pictures as 'friends' and 'not friendly' or 'hard to feel friendly with,' how would you choose among these eight pictures?"

Creating another set of columns, the teacher headed them "FRIENDLY" and "UNFRIENDLY." Under "UNFRIENDLY," the students selected "the one with people" (Seurat's *Sunday Afternoon on the Grand Jatte*), "the town with the blue churches and houses" (Delaunay's *Towers of Laon*), and "the tall shady trees" (Monet's *Poplars*).

Conclusion. The class of third and fourth graders gradually arrived at the insight that "yellow, orange, and red" are "easy to get close to and make you feel good," whereas colors in the "unfriendly" pictures were "too icy cold." (The dominant colors in those pictures ranged from ice-green to blue-violet.)

Shown a hue spectrum and color wheel, students noticed that green-blue-violet-purple were "a family," and that yellow-orange-red were another "family," opposite each other on the wheel. Further analysis and synthesis developed the insight that the yellow-red "family" was "warm feeling" whereas the green-purple "family" was "cold feeling." The students and their teacher freely associated and discussed

39

many things that "feel warm and friendly" in contrast with other things that "feel cool, are distant and unfriendly." They concluded that "green-purple family" pictures generally express cool, reserved, and distant feelings whereas "yellow-red family" pictures are exciting, inviting, and easy to feel close to. Each student then reflected upon a personal memory experience and depicted it with expressively appropriate warm or cool color schemes.

UPPER ELEMENTARY ART EXPERIENCES

Fifth and sixth graders are generally very open, enthusiastic, and capable when presented with qualitative learning opportunities. One such opportunity integrates different sensory perceptions and produces a work resulting from this integration. According to a dictionary definition, "synesthesia" is "a phenomenon in which one type of stimulation evokes the sensation of another, as the hearing of a sound resulting in the . . . visualization of a color" (*American Heritage*, 1973). The phenomenon is common and perhaps essential for the full experience of art. As Dewey asserted,

> Nothing is perceived except when different senses work in relation . . . except when the energy of one 'center' is communicated to others, and . . . new modes of motor responses are incited which in turn stir up new sensory activities. (16, p. 175)

There is ample evidence that mature visual artists have enjoyed and employed auditory-visual synesthesia. The pioneer abstract expressionist painter, Wassily Kandinsky, termed his synesthetic fusions of musical quality with color, shape, texture, and line quality "consonance" (51, p. 133). In his autobiography, he wrote of experiencing "the chiaroscuro of Rembrandt's paintings as 'a giant chord.' " Later, he experienced the "giant chord" of Rembrandt's painterly treatment of light in Wagner's use of trumpets in *Lohengrin*. In America, a number of twentieth century painters have explored audiovisual consonance. The fusion of jazz qualities with rhythms of color, shape, and line is evident in the paintings of Stuart Davis (who was a jazz connoisseur throughout his mature years as a New York artist) and in those of John Marin. Arthur G. Dove made a career of the abstract synthesis of auditory and visual qualities. His *Fog Horns* of 1929 (oil on canvas; Colorado Springs Fine Arts Center) exemplifies qualitative synthesis. And Morris Graves integrated mysterious qualities of moonlit bird song with

40

visual and tactual paint qualities in his gouache of 1939, *Bird Singing in the Moonlight* (Museum of Modern Art, New York City). Audiovisual synesthesia has also been demonstrated by contemporary photo and film artists.

The sample lesson that follows suggests how intermediate elementary students can problem solve and conceptualize by integrating their sensory channels of perception.

Fifth and sixth graders of an interdisciplinary visual arts program explored a range of cross-sensory qualitative integrations. They listened to varieties of musical rhythm and represented these auditory-kinesthetic perceptions in constructions of wire, multicolored and multi-shaped beads, yarn, and paper weavings and collages. They listened to and recorded qualitative differences in pitch, volume, and intensity in a variety of contexts. For instance, they recorded the comings and goings of truck and auto horns, police and street sirens, and they compared these with sounds of office and industrial machines. They converted these perceptions into two- and three-dimensional abstractions of line, color, texture, and shape.

One result of their synesthetic explorations was the translation of human vocal utterances into three-dimensional assemblages. Students first improvised a series of vocal expressions ranging from "grunts" and "slurps" to "shouts" and "screams." Posted words named the many vocal qualities that had been expressed. Then each student selected a word and contemplated possible visual, tactual, and kinetic representations of that particular vocal quality. Each student chose from a rich variety of assemblage materials. After 30 minutes of improvisatory work, individuals were asked to come to the front of the room to display their synesthetic constructions, expecting their peers to be able to match them with the vocal expressions they were intended to represent. The presentation of a 10-year-old boy was a plasticene cup with long, thin dowel sticks emanating from the rim in a radiating pattern. He marched to the front of the room, turned to face the group, stood erect, and held the cup in front of his mouth. The synesthetic perception "yell" was immediate and unanimous throughout the room.

Qualitative Interpretation of Ancient Cultures

A *qualitative* methodology for developing student rapport with peoples and value systems of other times and places uses and develops student abilities of metaphorical perception, comparison, and differentiation. Art educator Hermine Feinstein informs us how "metaphoric process can be used to interpret art periods"

41

(25, p. 28). She notes that every cultural epoch is marked by distinctive expressive forms that reflect primary conceptions, belief, and value systems of its people. "We can grasp the essence of a period," she states, "by making a tentative metaphor, an overarching grabber, to capture those characteristics and to direct us back to the parts...and then by asking...what do these works mean?" She demonstrates her qualitative method for cross-cultural studies as follows:

> Consider three periods of Greek art. Art of the Minoan period is known for its colorful and bold shapes, rhythmic and undulating motion, exuberance, grace and...naturalism. Art of the Mycenaean period is known for its stiffness and formality and its concern with war, hunting, and...fortifications. In stark contrast, art of the Classical period is known for its rationality, order, balance, harmony. (25, p. 28)

Feinstein believes that the three Greek epochs can be communicated and understood by metaphorical comparison and differentiation with the developmental stages of adolescence. Thus perhaps, American adolescents may develop rapport with ancient Greeks through metaphoric comparison of Greek art style progressions with progressions experienced in adolescent growth. A sample lesson in cultural interpretation follows.

An interdisciplinary team composed of art, English, and social studies teachers prepared a cultural inquiry experience for sixth graders by researching and selecting pictures of the characteristic art forms of two disparate cultures: Egyptian Old Kingdom, ca. 2500 B.C., and French mid-eighteenth century aristocratic rococo society. The students were presented a diversified array of pictures on two large panels at opposite ends of an art classroom. Egyptian culture was displayed on one panel and French cultural examples were shown on the opposing panel. No information whatsoever was given about the two divergent cultures. The interdisciplinary team members had agreed that the early provision of historical information would tend to distract or block student inquiry learning processes.

Modeling Cultural Qualities. Students were asked to scan each display, taking in the dominant qualities—of rhythmic pattern, of overall shape, of color, tonality, weight, texture, and line. After preliminary scanning, students were asked to decide individually or in teams which of the two displays to interpret by producing a "visual model" of its dominant qualities. They could choose from a rich variety of graphic, painting, and three-dimensional assemblage materials ranging from wires, strings, yarns to wood and plastic milling scraps, cloth, cotton, and styrofoam.

After a period of intensive qualitative analysis and interpretive reconstruction, each student or team presented a multisensory model for one of the displayed cultures. All teachers and students then took time to observe, compare, contrast, evaluate, and reflect upon the interpretive validity and communicative implications of each model.

Comparative Interpretation of Two Cultures. Through group interaction and discussion, the students came to terms with the various cultural representations. Two or three models were selected as the exemplars for each pictorial display. For French eighteenth century rococo culture the models were curvy, fluffy, and jiggly, whereas those for ancient Egypt were rectangular, boxy, and stiff. Easels with paper pads were placed beside each display and a teacher recorded student brainstorming of words and phrases appropriate to the major qualities that had been perceived and artfully composed to represent each display.

Discoveries and Conjectures. Playfully imaginative verbal brainstorming led to discoveries and conjectures about the two disparate cultures. For the rococo display, words included "silly," "wriggly," "curvy," "fluffy," "light," "flighty," "gay," "cheerful," and "fancy." For the Egyptian display students used "stiff," "rigid," "square," "straight," "'upright," "weighty," "heavy," and "serious." Asked to guess about lifestyles and value systems of the respective cultures, students hypothesized that members of rococo society liked to dance, play, and enjoy life rather than prepare for an afterlife, whereas members of Egyptian society were strict, disciplined, and preoccupied with an afterlife. Gradually, the teachers entered the discussion and added relevant information about French eighteenth century aristocratic society, philosophy, art, drama, government, and colonialism, and about the rule of ancient Egyptian pharoahs and priests and their elaborate preparations for an afterlife.

Near the end of the interdisciplinary art classtime, students intuited historically accurate perceptions of the relationship of "silly," "dizzy," and "free" forms to French eighteenth century philosophy, and the relationship of "serious," "rigid," and "disciplined" art forms to Egyptian culture and government. They concluded that the "free" forms of French aristocratic society relate to the spirit of liberty that was manifested by the American Revolution and Declaration of Independence of 1776 (and the later French Revolution that destroyed the French aristocracy), and that the rigidities of Egyptian art characterized a monolithic and totalitarian culture.

Students selected the word "dictatorship" at the conclusion of their qualitative analysis of Egyptian forms, and "freedom" at the end of their analysis of rococo forms. They also concluded with the insight that the typical art forms of a people can reveal an underlying system of beliefs and values. They agreed that "reading" the cultural art forms requires the skills of visual analysis and reconstruction that they had used in their study of French and Egyptian art.

MIDDLE SCHOOL/JUNIOR AND SENIOR HIGH SCHOOL ART EXPERIENCES

Given a school district's administrative and policy commitment to the development and enhancement of qualitative art abilities for all students, it is reasonable to expect junior and senior high school programs comparable in content, methodology, and resources to those specified for elementary art education.

Art educational contents and methodologies for junior and senior high school students may appropriately differ from elementary contents and procedures to the degree that adolescent interests and needs differ from those of young children. The openness and unstinting enthusiasm of the younger students for new realms of artistic experience often cannot be realistically expected of secondary level students. Their identities shaken by physical and psychological changes going on within, these students feel compelled to appear "cool" and jaded though they may not be. Thus, the junior and senior high art teacher may wisely hesitate to present fine art contents and tasks that appear either "childish" or unduly "artistic" to young adolescent students. Rather, the wise secondary-level educator focuses upon the straightforward communication and development of the prime characteristics of qualitative intelligence and knowledge that are identified in Chapter 1.

Thus, adolescent students are empowered to (1) *perceive* and represent in two- and three-dimensional art materials the basic visual, tactual, and spatial structures that infer meaning in cultural art objects; (2) *assimilate* the perceived basic expressive structures of cultural art objects with personal memory images; (3) *accommodate* the assimilated structures of cultural art expression and personal memory to new objects, environments, people, events, and subjects studied in school or encountered in everyday life; (4) *associate* feelings and values with the perceived, assimilated, and accommodated cultural forms and personal memories; and (5) skillfully *apply* these acquired perceptions, assimilations, accommodations, and associated feelings by producing original art work in various two- and three-dimensional media. Sample lessons for seventh and eighth graders follow.

Guernica

An audiovisual report of Pablo Picasso's process of creating the famous *Guernica* mural of 1937 was presented to a class of about 25 seventh graders. The report was prepared and presented as a slide-lecture by a junior high art teacher. Her primary source of historical information and photo-slide illustration was Rudolf Arnheim's 1962 publication *Picasso's Guernica, The Genesis of a Painting*.

Before the audiovisual report of Picasso's process, students were read a newspaper account of the infamous daylight bombing raid on the ancient Basque town of Guernica (London *Times*, April 27, 1937, cited in Arnheim [1, p. 18]). They heard that Nazi bombers dropped thousand-pound bombs and thousands of incendiary projectiles on the "open town far behind the lines" of the Spanish Civil War during a sunny April afternoon in 1937. They also heard that fighter planes "plunged low to machine-gun those of the civilian population who had taken refuge in the fields." Students then made pencil, crayon, felt-marker, and watercolor pictures of images that had been produced in their minds by the newspaper report.

At the beginning of their subsequent art period, the seventh graders viewed a display of all their sketches and paintings stimulated by the newspaper account of the Nazi raid on Guernica. In conjunction with the display, they viewed a large color reproduction of Picasso's *Guernica* painting. They were startled to discover no likenesses between their pictorial conceptions and Picasso's painting. Whereas they had pictured planes dropping bombs and incendiaries on a medieval Spanish town and machine-gunning frightened civilians who were fleeing into nearby fields during a sunny afternoon, Picasso showed a jagged pattern of lights and shadows depicting a night scene, lighted by flames, an oil lamp, and an electric bulb, with a screaming horse, a stoic bull, four terrified women (one with a dead child), and a smashed classical warrior statue. The students' task was to account for the discrepancy between their pictures, that were based on news reports, and Picasso's mural conception.

The art teacher projected a series of slide pictures of the sketches that led Picasso to his overall mural conception (1, pp. 31–116). Further, she showed a picture of his earlier *Minotauromachy* etching of 1935 (1, p. 4), and seven photographs of the mural in-process (pp. 119–28). She also showed slides of Picasso's many depictions of bulls, horses, and bullfighting scenes created before and after his 1937 conception of *Guernica*. Students quick-sketched their most memorable impressions and wrote notes next to the sketches clarifying what they had seen and heard while the audiovisual presentation was in progress. Their next task was to review and analyze what they had experienced and to hypothesize Picasso's reasons for painting something other than the news-reported event of April 26, 1937.

Student Conclusions. Through discussions focused upon many hunch-

45

es the students had expressed and the teacher had recorded and displayed on easel papers, the class consensually decided that Picasso had created and composed *symbols of human experience* rather than an illustration of an actual event. They agreed that *an artistic symbol* goes beyond the surface appearance of objects and events and reveals deeper human meanings and values. They decided that the underlying, humanistic value "statement" of Picasso's visual composition might be correctly restated as follows:

> The proud and heroic spirit of ancient Spain, that is symbolized by the majestic bull that protectively encircles a screaming mother and dead child, will not die but will protect, revive, and guide civilization through its present [1937] ordeal of Fascist violence. The light of enduring civilization is symbolized by the lamp thrust into the darkness and chaos by a concerned woman. The victimization of feminine human gentleness symbolized by the gored horse that Picasso remembered from traditional ritual slayings at Spanish bullfights, and the smashing of classical ideals of honorable warfare, symbolized by the shattered warrior statue, are tragic events of the present moment, but the lamplight and majestic bull provide reassurance and hope that humanity and civilization can and will survive.

Assimilation, Accommodation, and Association of Guernica Concepts. Each seventh grader was asked to remember a personal event or imagine a future event of her/his life that might relate to the main ideas and feelings symbolized in Picasso's *Guernica*. Words and phrases such as "proud and heroic spirit," "protect, revive, and guide civilization," "human gentleness," "smashing of classical ideals," and "reassurance and hope" were underlined to emphasize key ideas and values and to stimulate re-creative thinking. Each student wrote helpful notes to accompany his or her exploratory sketches of memory events or future happenings relevant to the *Guernica* conception.

Application of Guernica Ideas and Art Skills. With the help and advice of the art teacher, each student reviewed exploratory sketches, selected some for development into a single pictorial composition, experimented with compositional schemes, and then selected art media for a final production. The teacher facilitated these processes by reminding individuals of the extensive series of simple sketches and compositional trials that had preceded Picasso's "solution" of the *Guernica* mural "problem."

Outcomes. Each member of the class produced a large felt-marker, ink, paper-collage, and oil-pastel composition representing either a memory experience or an imagined future event that expressed at least one of the main ideas that the students had discovered in Picasso's *Guernica*. With the technical guidance of the art teacher, the remembered or imagined events were generalized into simplified symbolic figures (animal, human, machine, etc.). These bold, simple figures and their backgrounds were integrated into overall light and

46

dark compositional patterns that directed the eye among key pictorial elements to "tell a story" or "make a statement" in visual form. The seventh graders thus demonstrated and polished their abilities to convert personal experiences and imaginings into mythic, symbolic imagery, as had Picasso when he conceived and composed a mural representing some basic human values and meanings that had been challenged by the victimization of Guernica in 1937.

Interpreting Edward Hopper

A junior high school art educator projected an upside-down slide view of Edward Hopper's 1942 oil, *Nighthawks*, so that eighth graders were able to see only abstract color shapes and their overall pattern. On a teacher-prepared worksheet, students circled only word combinations that described expressive visual qualities that they saw in the abstracted, upside-down painting. (Among expressive pictorial qualities named on the worksheet were "wide rectangular picture," "harsh yellow spear," "pale green shaft," and "blackish-purple background." Most word clusters were unrelated to the slide projection.) After finishing this individualized perceptual exercise, students brainstormed their perceptions and selections of the most expressive visual qualities of the inverted slide projection. These student decisions were recorded on a large easel paper.

Abstracting Expressive Qualities. The teacher distributed colored papers cut to the rectangular shape and proportion of the slide projection. Using chalks and oil pastels, each student recreated the dominant color, line, shape, directional, and proportional qualities that had been selected through group brainstorming. Students turned their renderings around, as they worked, so that "the whitish-yellow spear" entered from the right and the "shark's nose-like pale blue shape" appeared at the lower left edge. Turning the slide projection around and into focus, the teacher revealed that students had rendered the basic shapes and colors of an oil painting that depicts a night scene in the city, with two customers at a counter in an all-night restaurant where the customers are served by a counterman in a white jacket and cap.

Students noticed and added pictorially meaningful shapes, colors, and details overlooked in the preliminary qualitative analysis. Using fine-tip felt markers, they sketched the man seated at the counter with his back toward the street, the two stainless-metal coffee makers that stand like sentinels against the starkly-lit restaurant wall, the triangular shaft of pale blue light on the man's felt hat—and the three blankly staring, dark-shadowed windows of the dark red wall above the distant storefront.

Evaluating Expressive Qualities. Recognizing that students generally lack a richly expressive interpretive language, the art teacher provided a "semantic differential" (cf. Chapter 1, Museum Gallery Tour, pp. 24–25) of interpretive and evaluative terminology that is characteristi-

47

cally used by artists and connoisseurs of art. The students individually rated the expressive features of Hopper's painting that seemed most meaningful to them. Their individual ratings were then compared and contrasted through a group discussion that generated many insights.

One student expressed his "hunch" that the picture means "harsh," "gloomy," and "threatening." Other students agreed and offered "evidence" to confirm a "harsh-gloomy-threatening" interpretation, enriching it with "lonesome" and "isolated." They said that "harshness" is expressed by the stark whitish-yellow "spear," by the pale blue shaft of light on the sidewalk that counterbalances a whitish-yellow, pale green, fluted column in the restaurant's rounded-window corner, and by a harsh Irish-green window counter with the stark-yellow interior wall and ceiling. Students noted that there is something "grating" abut the contrast of whitish-yellow with intense green and the pale blue shaft or light. They also perceived that the somewhat lighter triangle of blue in the distant, storefront window and in the male customer's felt hat "grates" against the whitish-yellow and intense green. The sharp "spear" shapes throughout the composition express both "harshness" and a sense of "threatening." They also noted that the individuals in the restaurant are "isolated" from each other and, significantly, from the viewers of the work. Students commented, too, on the quality of extreme quiet throughout the painting, the separating wall of glass, and the fact that backs and faces of pictured individuals are all turned away from the viewers.

At the end of the class, students discussed how Hopper's title *Nighthawks* adds metaphoric meaning. Later, they did library research on Hopper and the post-Depression, World War II era. They explained connections between the spirit of that cultural epoch and the art styles it spawned. They reflected upon personal memory experiences that relate to the qualities of *Nighthawks* and were encouraged to produce individually original pictures expressive of these recollections.

Transfiguring the Commonplace

According to philosophers and art educators cited in Chapter 1, a primary psychological and social function of arts experience is to release the individual from the dullness and anesthesia of everyday life and the limitations of stereotypical perception and thought. The artist, according to Randall, reveals "unsuspected qualities" in ordinary things, "enhancing the significance" of everyday existence (47). Art vivifies what we have "encountered before but not seen" (17, p. 12) and is "the transfiguration of the commonplace" (33, p. 129). Therefore, a prime goal of high school art education is to release the student from the anesthesia of routinized and standardized existence. The sample lessons that follow were designed to help senior high school students break out of anesthetized attitudes and conceptions of ordinary experience. In the first example, students discovered unforeseen magic in their everyday school environment.

Discovering the Extraordinary in the Ordinary

The high school art teacher projected slide sequences showing Claude Monet's *Haystack Series* of 1890–91, *Rouen Cathedral Series* of 1894, *Poplars* suite of 1891, *Houses of Parliament* seen across the Thames, *Piazza San Marco* viewed across Venetian waters, 1904–08, and extensive studies of Monet's lily pond and Japanese footbridge at Giverny. Teacher and students read and highlighted interpretive writings of critic Gustave Geffroy, of the artist's own epoch, who commented that Monet's paintings express the "sensation of the fleeting instant, which has just come to life, dies and will not return," and "reveal the infinite changes of time on the eternal phase of nature" (28). Monet's Cathedral and Poplars series "lead us to abstraction." Geffroy found them "suspended in time," and ghostlike." As for the Giverny lily pond studies, Geffroy wrote that they are "vaporous . . . ephemeral unions . . . grasping for the immaterial . . . without form or depth at the verge of abstraction'" (28).

Reminding students that Monet attended with great concentration to the passage of time in an ordinary hayfield, along the banks of an ordinary river, and in his own backyard, the teacher asked them to give comparable attention to transcience "at the verge of abstraction" within their high school building.

The Extraordinary Swimming Pool. For several weeks, one high school senior regularly visited the high school swimming pool and, occasionally, the resource center, to capture qualities of transcience. Returning to the art studio, she produced studies and improvisations in many media. She used cuttings of gray, white, and black papers to shape a collage; she used charcoal, watercolor, ink, colored scraps of paper, and screen wire, strung wires, straws, and toothpicks to express undulations and rhythms of pool waters and high school swimmers and divers moving in the waters. Her multimedia productions moved back and forth from realistic depiction to sensory abstraction. At the end of several weeks of sustained inquiry and improvisation, the student prepared and presented a "retrospective exhibition" within the high school building. Her works were worthy of the critical commentary that the works of Monet generated from Geffroy. Through her perceptively creative processes she had arrived at "a meeting of minds" with a master artist and a master critic of painting. (Lesson by James Hall, Attleboro High School, Massachusetts)

Breaking the Boundaries of Perception

Henry David Thoreau exemplifies the breaking of conventionalized boundaries of perception and conception. To examine the mysteries of the universe, he settled for a year on the banks of a pond in his hometown. There, he detected processes and patterns that are fundamental and pervasive throughout the universe. Among his discoveries was a flowing and branching pattern that evolved before his eyes in an ordinary sandbank one March morning, which he described in the chapter entitled "Spring" of *Walden*. He speculated that the pattern is one of the basic organizing principles of all existence. As he described his experience:

> Innumerable little streams overlap and interlace . . . exhibiting a sort of hybrid product, which obeys halfway the law of currents, and halfway that of vegetation. As it flows it takes the forms of sappy leaves or vines . . . you are reminded of coral, of leopards' paws, of birds' feet, of brains or lungs. . . .
>
> I am affected as if in a peculiar sense I stood in the laboratory of the Artist who made the world and me. . . . No wonder the earth expresses itself outwardly in leaves, it so labors with the idea inwardly. . . . The feathers and wings of birds are . . . drier and thinner leaves. . . . The very globe continually transcends and translates itself. . . . Even ice begins with delicate crystal leaves. . . . The whole tree itself is but one leaf, and rivers are still vaster leaves whose pulp is intervening earth, and towns and cities are the ova of insects in their axils. (56)

Following Thoreau's lead, a high school art teacher planned and conducted a boundary-beaking, metaphoric experience for ninth and tenth graders.

The Extraordinary Leaf

After audition and discussion, the art teacher directed student attention to the final sentence of the passage from *Walden* in which Thoreau likens the whole pattern of trees and river drainage systems to a single leaf with "its pulp" seen as "intervening earth," and imagines cities and towns as insect eggs laid at the intersections of leaf veins and stems. Given these metaphoric images, students were asked to find relevant leaf forms for use in later art classes.

During subsequent classes, freshman and sophomore students worked diligently upon large multimedia drawings of the leafy forms brought to class. Some worked from cabbage leaves, others from grape or maple leaves. They imaginatively rendered the ridges and valleys of "intervening earth" among leaf veins. They graphically textured various surface qualities as though studied with a magnifying glass. At the joints of branches and veins, they elaborated Thoreau's "towns and cities" that are "ova of insects in their axils." During these art classes, students described the interrelationships they perceived between various leaf forms and the geography of rivers and urban centers within their region. Some students elaborated the "rivers" and "tributary streams" into transportation systems, depicting river-going vessels of all types, harbors and wharves, bridges and roadways. (Lesson by Norman Nilsen, Attleboro High School, Massachusetts)

These high school students discovered the extraordinary in ordinary leaves, extending their perceptions to many other contexts of experience. Other high school students discovered the extraordinary in ordinary *holes*.

Discovering the Qualitativeness of Holes

Students took their lead from the American painter, Georgia O'Keeffe, and from British sculptor, Henry Moore. They listened to two recorded statements, the first by O'Keeffe, the second by Moore:

I was the sort of child that ate around the raisin on the cookie and ate around the hole in the doughnut.... So probably—not having changed much—when I started painting the pelvic bones I was most interested in the holes in the bones—what I saw through them—particularly the blue from holding them up in the sun against the sky.... They were most wonderful against the Blue—the Blue that will always be there. (44)

Pebbles show Nature's way of working stone. Some of the pebbles I pick up have holes right through them.

A piece of stone can have a hole through it and not be weakened.... On the principle of the arch it can remain just as strong....

A hole can itself have as much shape-meaning as a solid mass.

Sculpture in air is possible, when the stone contains only the hole, which is the intended and considered form.

The mystery of the hole—the mysterious fascination of caves in hillsides and cliffs. (41, p. 75)

As students listened to the statements of the two artists, they examined reproductions of three paintings by O'Keeffe and photographs of four works by Moore. The O'Keeffe paintings were *Pelvis with Moon* (1943, 30" x 24"), *Pelvis III* (1944, 48" x 40"), and *Pelvis Series, Red with Yellow* (1945, 36" x 48"). The Moore works were *Reclining Figure* (1939, Elmwood), *Sculptural Object* (1960, bronze), *Reclining Mother and Child* (1960–61, bronze), and *Double Oval* (1966, marble).

51

Students expressed these and other insights about artistic imagination and creativity:

"The 'hole' is not just empty and meaningless, it can be as expressive as solid forms."

"A hole in a pelvic animal bone, an eroded beach pebble, or sculpture forms a kind of frame through which a world beyond is 'captured' for appreciative attention."

"The framed 'world beyond' can been seen as positive 'figure' rather than 'background'."

"The positive hole or cavity provokes metaphorical imagery; for instance, O'Keeffe's eternal 'Blue,' and Moore's 'caves' of imagination."

Stimulated by these concepts, students went to find natural forms with "expressive holes." Some visited butchers and retrieved throwaway animal parts. Others found dried root structures and the kind of beach-eroded forms alluded to by Moore. Using their found objects, students made a variety of re-presentations in conventional and unconventional art media. They produced charcoal and ink drawings, watercolor and tempera paintings, plasticene and moist-clay models, papier-mâché, screen wire, and plaster gauze compositions, and carvings of various woods.

Students moved conceptually from the distanced stance of a remote observer to that of a person consumed by the hole.

Two final tasks were given: (1) View something *through* the hole, as O'Keeffe viewed the sky, and make that thing the "positive" of your artwork (as O'Keeffe made a golden egg of the hole in *Pelvis Series, Red with Yellow*); and (2) Conceive of yourself as a tiny, insignificant creature "lost" within the expansive opening (as though under a monumental natural bridge).

During a summative critique surrounded by their many studies and improvisations, students agreed that they had acquired a new appreciation of the creative thought processes of two exemplary artists, a sense of the connectedness of things in the natural world, and an appreciation of their own abilities for finding qualitative meaning in common things. (Lesson by James Hall and Norman Nilsen, Attleboro High School, Massachusetts)

SUMMARY: QUALITATIVE LESSON FORMAT

The sample lessons given in the preceding pages may be generalized into a qualitative teaching process as shown in Figure 1.

Figure 1
Qualitative Art Lesson

I. Teacher presentation of objects for perceptual interpretation

II. Student group interaction with presented objects
  A. Elicitation of metaphoric language about the salient qualities of the objects
  B. Elicitation of quick sketches, in various art media, of salient qualities perceived in the objects
  C. Group discussion, leading to consensus about the salient expressive features of the objects

III. Individual student improvisations of personal imagery relevant to the objects
  A. Quick sketches, in various art media, of recalled experiences having qualities similar to the salient expressive features seen in the objects (Activity II)

IV. Contextual inquiry and decision making
  A. Teacher presentation of facts and examples from the historical, cultural, stylistic and/or intellectual contexts of the objects; student research and reporting
  B. Student quick-sketching, in various media, of contextual "facts" (i.e., images) that, to each student, are most like the salient features identified in Activity II

V. Individual student production of a relevant art object
  A. Student selection of sketches, metaphors, and facts from prior activities (II–IV) for synthesis in an original art production
  B. Production, teacher-assisted as needed, of an object re-presenting (in art media of student choice) the student's "main idea" (synthesis of salient features) of the objects studied (Activities II–IV)

VI. Lesson closure
  A. Exhibition of student products
  B. Group discussion
    1. Comparison and contrast of salient features seen in student works and the originally presented objects
    2. Summation: Consensus about the main ideas discovered and recorded, in artworks and metaphoric language, as a consequence of the teacher-guided lesson.

Chapter 3

INTERDISCIPLINARY QUALITATIVE ART EDUCATION

RATIONALE

The qualitative way of perceiving, thinking, and knowing that is developed through inductive and constructive processes of effective school art education should not be limited to the visual arts program. As Dewey claims, the "logic of artistic construction and aesthetic appreciation is peculiarly significant because they exemplify in accentuated and purified form" (15, p. 103) a mode of thought and ideation, guided throughout by intuition of "underlying pervasive quality" (p. 112), that "is the background, the point of departure, and the regulative principle of *all* thinking (p. 116, emphasis added). Given the universal need for experiences of "artistic construction and aesthetic appreciation" (i.e., *qualitative experiences*) to undergird, as Dewey claims, all so-called higher or more abstract forms of thought and knowledge, it is appropriate to extend art education to all the subjects of schooling.

INTERDISCIPLINARY ART IN PRIMARY GRADES

Qualitative art educational principles and methods can help students master a variety of skills and concepts in language, mathematics, science, social studies, and other basic subjects (e.g., music). At primary grade levels, for instance, arts specialists have demonstrated the rhythmic patterning of sentences by performing corresponding rhythmic sequences on kettledrums and by articulating the same linear patterns with variously colored and shaped beads strung along wires. Visual art educators have helped students perceive "baselines," "peaks," and "valleys" in syllabic configurations, comparing their word-configuration perceptions with pictures of mountain ranges. Subsequently, students joined a music teacher in rhythmic clapping and melodic singing of observed "peaks," "valleys," and "rests" of displayed word, phrase, and sentence lines.

54

To help second graders differentiate vowels and consonants, an art specialist gave them smooth (acetate film) and rough (sandpaper) squares and rectangles. She called the smooth shapes "vowels" and the rough shapes "consonants." Given choices of four- and five-letter words (e.g., *word, open, glass, house*), each child reconstructed the words as tactile "peak, baseline, or valley" shape-sequences. When the second graders had finished choosing, positioning, and glueing "texture words," they engaged in games of matching visual-tactile constructions with teacher-posted and spoken words. In this way, they discovered their capacities for translating abstract qualitative patterns into actual words and phrases.

Subsequent to textural and configurational experiences with syllabication, third-graders made "syllable animals." For instance, a student first analyzed and texture-blocked appropriate syllabic structures for "gi-raffe" and "rab-bit." Asked to "mix up" syllabic animal word parts, the third grader combined "rab" and "raffe" forming "rab-raffe." Faced with this unusual animal name, the child constructed a new creature by combining and integrating rabbit features with giraffe features. Upon completion of "syllabic animal" pictures in crayon, felt marker, or oil pastel colors, the many child-created "sylly animals" were exhibited throughout the school building. A written syllabic "mixup" was displayed under each unusual animal depiction to inform others of the basis for the original animal conception. (Lesson by Mary Sumner Antaya, Finberg Elementary School, Attleboro, Massachusetts)

To help third graders with phonetic decoding skills, an interdisciplinary art facilitator designed and implemented the lesson that follows.

The Poor Little Vowel That Can't Say its Name

To reinforce the phonetic generalization that a vowel enclosed between consonants has the "short" sound, third-graders were asked to represent a situation in which a "poor, weak, timid vowel" is "trapped" between two "strong and strict" consonants and, thus constrained, "can't even say its name" (its long sound). Given art paper 12 inches high and 18 inches wide with a teacher-made vertical fold-back at its center, each student watercolored a large, lower-case vowel shape across the fold. To the right and left of the vowel, each student brushed a large, lower-case consonant shape (e.g., *h* and *t* enclosing the vowel *a*). Using various graphic media, each student then pictured the enclosed vowel as weak and timid and the enclosing consonants as strong and unyielding.

On paper 12 inches high and 6 inches wide, each student brushed an *e* of relatively the same size, color, and placement as the "timid vowel" pictured across the fold of the 12 by 18-inch paper. Each student then pictorially elaborated the *e*-shape with "strong and silent" imagery. A piece of masking tape was attached, extending with sticky side up from the underside of the "*e*-ending."

How the Timid Vowel Became Brave. Enacting the tale of "the timid vowel that can't say its own name" until given courage by a "silent *e,*" each third grader stood before the class and, while pronouncing the consonant-vowel-consonant word correctly, pulled the tape-attached "silent-*e*" paper to stretch open the previously folded 12 by 18-inch paper. As *hat,* or *rob,* or *rat* was lengthened by the pull of the *e*-ending, the enclosed vowel (previously pictured over a fold) lengthened too. Suddenly, the enclosed and constrained vowel was revealed as "long" (physically widened). After displaying and correctly pronouncing the new four-letter word (e.g., *hate, robe,* or *rate*), each student added pictorial features on the underfold that helped show how the previously constrained and "timid" vowel had become both "long" and "strong."

Each class member had experienced the plight of consonant-enclosed vowels and the significance of attached "silent-*e* endings" by making a difficult, abstract phonetic concept concrete and personal.

To qualitatively reinforce a spelling rule, another interdisciplinary specialist devised the following "visual learning" device.

Finding the Plural Form of Words Ending with y

To illustrate the complex principle that "when a singular word ends in a *y* after a consonant, it is changed to a plural word by converting the *y* to *i* and adding *es,*" the teacher invented an instructional foldout card for picturing and enacting the "*y* to *ies*" rule. Picturing a singular word with a *y* ending (e.g., baby) on the major area of the card, and an *es* on the right fold of the card, the inventive teacher made the *y* of the left card fold transformable by constructing it of three cut-paper bars. A small brass fastener was passed through a hole at the top of the lower vertical bar and holes at the bottom of the other two bars. When fastened, the two bars could be spread to form a *v*-shape, or closed to form a vertical elongation of the lower bar. This transformable piece was inserted through two horizontal slits at the upper right of the left card fold. See the illustration that follows.

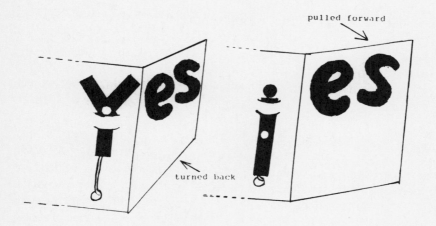

Then, the end of a length of string was firmly glued to the rear of the bottom bar of the transformable piece. When the glue was dry, the string was inserted through a punched hole at bottom right of the left card fold. With the transformable piece in the *y*-shape, and with the right card fold turned back (see illustration), the other end of the string was firmly taped to the far right rear of the right card fold.

When the right fold of the card was pulled forward, revealing the *es* lettering and the student's pictorial conception of the plural *ies* word meaning (e.g., the idea of babies), the taped string pulled down the transformable *y* to make it become a single upright bar. Above the vertical bar, a dot appeared (which had been concealed by the upper part of the prior *y*). Thus, an *i* appeared, as if magically, where a *y* had been.

INTERDISCIPLINARY COLLABORATION AT OTHER GRADE LEVELS

When assigned the role of "interdisciplinary" rather than "regular" visual art teacher, the teacher generally does not teach *the content* of the art field but is expected to extend *the process of* the artist to nonartistic subject matters. Functioning beyond the boundaries of the self-contained and intrinsically valuable discipline of art, the interdisciplinary art educator seeks content from other subjects that can be treated artistically. The rationale is that "art" is essentially a creative *process of qualification* (cf. Randall [47], Chapter 1) rather than an inert body of knowledge to be consumed by passive students. According to the theories of art and art

57

education that underlie this monograph, "art" is a "mind-altering" activity (23) of transforming the data of sensory experience into memorable imagery that is full of feeling. This imagery is inherently interdisciplinary since, as Dewey (14) and Broudy (9) inform us, it constitutes an allusionary base for thinking, interpreting, knowing, and problem solving in all the disciplines of human inquiry, knowledge, and value.

In qualitative interdisciplinary programs, *the integrity of art* continues as the hands-on and eyes-on *creative process of forming conceptual imagery* (i.e., of shaping imaginative forms of knowledge through active experience). Most important is the preservation, facilitation, and enhancement of imaginative art abilities for acquiring and using knowledge—of English, science, history and geography, mathematics, or music. Interdisciplinary art educators have a responsibility to maintain the integrity of perceptive and imaginative art-sensing and art-making processes as they help students master many diverse educational contents and disciplines of mind.

The interdisciplinary art teacher consults those who are knowledgeable and competent in non-art subjects to determine what *particular conceptualizations* students need to acquire, through art processes, in English or science, social studies, music or mathematics. Using this specific information, the art teacher plans *to transform* the non-art conceptual content and disciplines into imaginative art procedures and innovative art products (e.g., sculptures that articulate "math facts").

Examples

Multiplication Lesson

An interdisciplinary visual art teacher was asked by sixth-grade classroom teachers to plan and implement ways of enhancing student competencies in multiplication and student use of a multiplication table to solve problems coordinating longitude and latitude. The art educator distributed graph papers to all sixth graders and asked them to serially number from 1 to 10 a horizontal row and a vertical column of half-inch squares. She then asked them to calculate and write in the remaining 81 numbers of the 100-square area—finding each number by multiplying a number in the top row by its coordinated number in the vertical column.

58

When the sixth graders had finished numbering their multiplication tables, the art teacher asked each student to select one number from 2 to 10 and, with fine-tip markers, to color in every numbered square that was an even multiple of the selected number. As students completed this task, she questioned them about the evolving color patterns of their grids. Several students remarked that they had discovered "regular patterns" and "balanced designs." A few students who complained that they were not achieving "regular designs" soon realized that these irregularities were caused by their own calculating errors. They recognized that coloring in the correctly calculated squares would generate regular patterns, whereas incorrect calculations inevitably generated irregular patterns. Sharing this perception with classmates, all students carefully checked and corrected their choices of squares in their multiplication tables. (Lesson by Donna G. Smith, Coelho Middle School, South Attleboro, Massachusetts)

Adaptation of Multiplication Lesson to Cultural Arts

When an art teacher and a social studies teacher from another middle school visited the sixth-grade classrooms and saw the colorfully patterned math tables that had been produced, these teachers decided to adapt and extend the concepts and procedures of the sixth-grade lesson to cultural arts education at the seventh-grade level in their school.

Inventing Multiple Creature Features. After providing every seventh grader with the opportunity to discover regular patterns in correctly calculated and numbered multiplication tables, the art and social studies teachers transformed the math tables into devices for prescribing imaginary "multiple creature features." The teachers gave each student a grid with 100 squares and fanciful "creature feature" names written above and below each of the grid's 10 columns. For example, above column 1 (first column, left side), the teachers had written "ears" and below that column they had written "noses" (see sample grid, illustrated below).

After calculating, locating, and writing in all the numbers of a 100-square multiplication table, students were taught to apply the mathematical thinking process that had been successfully used by sixth-graders at the other middle school.

Students then were asked to select and circle 10 "creature features," either from those written above or below each column of the grid. They were to incorporate this inventory of features into a pictured "multiple-features creature." Before proceeding with this task, they were directed to calculate and record (see illustrated "features" inventory) a particular number of features for each student's distinctive picture.

Each student selected *an even number* from the top row of the multiplication table to use as the key determinate of the creature features

59

inventory. Using that number, each one searched *down*, from the circled words above the columns, and *up*, from the circled words below the columns, to find and *circle the first multiple of the even key number*. The ten circled numbers were then transposed to the inventory sheet. (The sample shows the inventory of a student who had selected the key number 6).

To complete the inventorying process, each student selected a divisor that could be used to divide her/his key number evenly. For instance, a student whose key was 8 chose the divisor 2, and a student whose key was 10 selected the divisor 5. Students completed the process by dividing their 10 circled and listed feature numbers by the divisor, and listing the products in the right column of the "creature features inventory" (see illustration). This was a "prescription" or "recipe" for the next task: the pictorial improvisation of a multifeatured creature composed of the number of features found in the left and right columns of the inventory sheet.

Sample Grid and Inventory

features	number	÷ by 3
ears	6	2
wings	18	6
arms	30	10
eyes	12	4
hands	30	10
horns	6	2
fangs	42	14
heads	24	8
mouths	72	24
hats	30	10

Multiple Creature Features in Oriental Cultures. To provide an art historical context for invention of multifeatured, fantasy creatures, the seventh graders were shown slides of Hindu and Buddhist sculptural deities with many heads, limbs, and gestures. Students were made aware of the compositional cohesiveness and the religious meanings of the Far Eastern deity objects. They were urged to thoughtfully plan the composition of a many-featured creature within the format of an 18- x 24-inch sheet of white art paper.

Every seventh grader in the school produced a richly elaborated multiple-features creature. These compositions exhibited surprising visual cohesiveness, given the large number of conventionally unrelated creature features that had been calculated for each pictorial composition. The student depictions were displayed prominently in the middle school building and were universally admired for their visual richness, their relevance to Oriental art, and their mathematically determined structures. The mathematical bases for artistic elaboration of creature features generated special interest and enthusiasm among science teachers of the building. (Lesson by Rena N. Bidney, Brennan Middle School, Attleboro, Massachusetts)

When interdisciplinary teaching methodologies are respected and encouraged throughout a school district, cross-disciplinary ideas and practices catch fire among teachers. This was the case in the district where the sixth-grade exercise in visual multiplication patterning led to the seventh-grade creature features project related to Hindu and Buddhist art. Further, the display of artistically pleasing and historically relevant multiple-feature creatures led to a new and exciting way of teaching taxonomical classification concepts and skills. The science teachers asked the collaborating art and social studies teachers to facilitate the transformation of imaginative math and cultural art experiences into valid and disciplined seventh-grade science education.

Extension to Science Education

The science educators recognized the extensive display of multiple creatures as a kind of zoological find in their midst. Using the artistic creations as subjects for biological classification, they taught their seventh graders to inventory the various kinds and numbers of features that constituted the many depictions. Students were taught to form taxonomical categories ranging from "class," "order," and "family," to "genus" and "species." They learned to assign the many exhibited creatures to the various categories according to the quantities of detec-

61

table features. In accordance with scientific convention, and guided by charts of Latin terminology and appropriate scientific usages, the students assigned Latin word clusters to each identified subspecies. These seventh graders were delighted by the impressive scientific names that were appropriately assigned to their art creations.

Another example of interdisciplinary collaboration among visual art and science educators follows.

Art and Atomic Science

The interdisciplinary visual art specialist asked each student to select one element from the Periodic Table for representation with various qualities of yarn stitched on a 10- by 10-inch square of burlap. She asked students to research atomic facts about their elements with science teachers. Armed with scientific and mathematical knowledge about a chemical element, each student was stimulated and guided by art and science teachers to improvise an abstract or pictographic image that correctly represented scientific fact but was not a copy or imitation of any standard scientific representation. A science educator reminded students that no one has ever seen an atom; therefore, all conventional models were imaginative speculations by intellectually informed scientists. He emphasized the role of improvisatory imagination in science. After each student had produced an original graphic image that a science teacher agreed was a valid representation of the atomic structure of a specific element, the art specialist provided the student with a 10- by 10-inch wooden frame and a square of colored or plain burlap. First, students viewed a slide show about fabric artistry. Then, selecting yarns, strings, threads and needles, they transferred their graphic conceptions into stitchery, stretching and tacking the burlap piece to a frame.

Upon completion of the individual pieces, groups of students arranged the framed units in patterns conforming to principles of atomic periodicity (i.e., they formed valid periodic tables). Then students turned the individual fabric pieces face down and proceeded to bind them together by stringing wires through holes in the wooden frames and stapling all the units to a large cardboard. Turned about, the fabric units were attractively composed into tapestry-like displays that were artistic presentations of scientific knowledge. (Lesson by Janice P. Newman, Thacher Middle School, Attleboro, Massachusetts)

From the preceding lesson samples, it is evident that interdisciplinary educators need to meet for the exchange of ideas and cross-fertilization of instructional strategies. Ideally, there is administrative provision for interdisciplinary planning. More realistically, planning is "catch as catch can." Interdisciplinary ideas and practices are exchanged through animated discussions during lunch periods or just before and at the end of the school day. Often, as demonstrated by the sequence that began with multiplication tables and ended with scientific taxonomies, cross-disciplinary ideas are circulated and promoted by means of classroom and building displays.

Art educators can be differentially assigned. Part of such an art specialist's day or week may be specifically reserved for interdisciplinary functioning, with other time reserved for self-contained visual arts education. Interdisciplinary functioning can be further differentiated into specific times for (1) meeting with teachers of other disciplines, (2) imaginative conversion of specific non-art content into qualitative processes and product-ideas, and (3) communication of non-art content to students through qualitative art processes that generate unusual art representations of non-art ideas, procedures, and values.

Effective interdisciplinary functioning requires an open and improvisatory attitude and style of all participants. The effective cross-disciplinary educator eagerly seeks out "grist for the mill" of integrative teaching and learning. Often "the grist" is without intrinsic artistic appeal. It is the task and the opportunity of the art specialist, however, to transform any such aesthetically neutral content into creative student learning procedures and outcomes that are qualitatively pleasing, enlivening, and fulfilling. Some examples of the transformation of unartistic into artistic processes and products follow.

Qualitative Transformation of Basic Sight Words

The interdisciplinary art specialist's task was to transform an aesthetically unappealing list of intermediate elementary basic sight words into educational activities and outcomes of creative and aesthetic quality.

In advance of the interdisciplinary art class, the art teacher prepared (1) a cardboard template for goggles of average fourth grade head size, (2) sheets of colored film, (3) thin sheets of copy board, pencils, markers, scissors, glue and tape, and (4) a placard displaying all the basic sight words prescribed for fourth-grade level.

As groups of students entered the art educator's room, they found him wearing colorful cardboard goggles. The teacher asked them to

63

look closely at the eyepieces as he walked among them. They detected the word "ocean" on each eyepiece. They saw that the goggles had been elaborated into images of ocean waves and creatures. Students remarked that the "glasses" "mean what they look like."

Each student (1) acquired a 6- by 16-inch card, (2) traced the "glasses" template onto the card, (3) selected a basic sight word, (4) researched word meaning, (5) pencil-designed an imaginative interpretation of the selected word's meaning, (6) pictorially elaborated the word meaning with marker colors, (7) cut the pictorially elaborated goggles from the card, folding it into wearable glasses, (8) cut out eye openings, (9) attached colored film eyepieces, (10) lettered the sight word in each eyepiece, and (11) wore "sight word glasses," displaying both the pictorial elaboration and lettered words.

Wearing their "sight-word goggles," students looked like a group of revelers at a masked ball or a tribe of sorcerers participating in a ritual conclave. They peered at each other through the "magic glasses," reading each other's words. Most students wore their "sight-word goggles" throughout the school day. The whole school was enlivened by students in "magic glasses," interacting, and thereby acquiring a wealth of basic word spellings and meanings. (Lesson by Stephen E. Saunders, Hill-Roberts Elementary School, South Attleboro, Massachusetts)

Qualification of Adjectives

Fifth graders were seated before a large panel displaying (1) photographs of imaginative furniture pieces by Samaras and Nevelson, surrealist boxes by Cornell, and pictures of a museum exhibition of elaborately decorated jewelry boxes; (2) definitions of "adjectives" and "transformation"; (3) lists of adjectives under *color, texture, size, shape, and appearance*; and (4) an assignment: "Collect an adjective from each set; find materials having the adjective's quality; combine them into a personal box sculpture."

After group discussion about the exhibited fantasy furniture and boxes and the categories of adjectives, each student went to the categorical lists, selected an adjective from each list, recorded them, and then searched among sensory materials for those that seemed to match the qualities of the five adjectives selected. Then each student went to a private working area and imaginatively constructed the five adjectival qualities into a personal box sculpture.

The products were innovative and expressive. The student who had selected "medium" size, "blue-white" color, "shaggy" texture, "floppy" shape, and "fluffy" appearance, had glued blue foil to a box 4 inches square and 1 inch deep. On the blue foil were strips of paper doily; white wafers; masses of yellow, orange, red, and white yarn forming a fluffy beard all around; and pink elastics. Another, who had selected "small," "colorful," "fuzzy," "fancy," and "light," presented a very delicate, tiny square box covered with soft white cotton and bound, in a pleasing pattern, with multicolored lengths of pipe cleaner. *Outcome.* The fifth graders were able to differentiate and use five different adjectival categories. They were able to match sensory materials with words selected from each category, and they were able to integrate the five distinctive qualities into a unitary box sculpture. In so doing, they identified their creative selves with famous contemporary artists, thus acquiring pride and confidence for future art endeavors. Students also gained recognition and appreciation of some of the interests and intentions of famous artists, as well as a realization that these interests and intentions can be applied to such commonplace objects as the words they encounter and use everyday in school. (Lesson by Stephen E. Saunders, Hill-Roberts Elementary School, South Attleboro, Massachusetts)

Geography and Human Anatomy

Fourth graders were seated before a large panel displaying (1) a placard defining "topography" as "the science of making accurate and detailed descriptions or drawings of geographical areas or regions, including surface features"; (2) a sign labeled "Body Maps," with a statement of how analogies can be drawn between topographical features and human anatomical features; (3) charts differentiating and defining land and water forms; (4) anatomy charts; and (5) vocabularies of landforms, water forms (e.g., *bay* and *fjord*), and human anatomical features and organs.

The interdisciplinary art specialist engaged students in a discussion of outline drawing of human anatomy and positions of the figure that can produce differing "maps." The teacher and students also discussed the sciences of geography and topography and their similarities and differences with physiology and anatomy.

Procedure

1. Students formed teams of two.
2. Teams collected 10 land or water formation words on index cards. They investigated topographical word meanings in dictionaries and on globes, maps, and charts.
3. Teams decided how to shape a body position on paper so that its outline would feature most of the collected and defined words.
4. One member of a team positioned her/his body on 24- by 36-inch white vellum paper; the other member penciled the body outline.
5. Delegating responsibilities, each team used felt-tip markers, wax, and oil crayons to thoroughly "map" a water or land region, incorporating at least eight of the indexed vocabulary word meanings into the map.

6. Team members added specific water or land facilities (e.g., railroad systems, airports, terminals, highway "arteries," river boats, and docks).
7. Teams labeled all topographical features and functional facilities with analogical compound words (e.g., "arm-pit bay," "elbow peninsula," "stomach swamp," or "digestion canal").
8. All teams presented their detailed and labeled "body maps" for educational display throughout the school building.

Educational Outcomes. Fourth graders selected and used topographical forms and their names to form and imaginatively elaborate "body map" pictorial analogies. They improvised transportation "terminals" and travel networks that are analogous to human organs and circulatory systems. Then they invented compound words that integrate topographical and anatomical vocabularies.

Through teamwork, students demonstrated cooperative learning skills. They identified their procedures with those of mapmakers and anatomical artists, thus gaining confidence and esteem associated with those adult competencies. They also demonstrated artistic abilities of metaphorical visualization and improvisation. (Lesson by Stephen E. Saunders, Hill-Roberts Elementary School, South Attleboro, Massachusetts)

The foregoing lessons illustrate ways that interdisciplinary visual art educators can function effectively within comprehensive schools. Through their example, other teachers and administrators can begin to transform the often aesthetically sterile content and procedures of ordinary schooling into qualitative experiences. Thus, can art permeate an educational environment and all teachers and administrators help "to restore continuity between the refined and intensified forms of experience that are works of art and the everyday events, doings, and sufferings that are universally recognized to constitute experience" (16, p. 3). Such acts of restoration and continuity between the ordinary and the aesthetic dimensions of human existence help affirm, with Dewey (15, p. 93), that "the world in which we immediately live, . . . strive, succeed, and are defeated is preeminently a qualitative world."

Chapter 4

EVALUATING QUALITATIVE ART EDUCATION

All teachers who are committed to the implementation of qualitative art instruction are well advised to plan and use methods and instruments for monitoring the quality of both the implementation and the educational outcomes of such a program. School boards need factual information about the benefits to be gained from the expenditures they authorize on behalf of any program. Art educators therefore would do well to systematically gather and present facts that will help the policymaking boards and their administrators make informed decisions on behalf of the qualitative education of students.

CLARIFYING PROGRAM GOALS

Evaluation is a process for determining the validity of the claims that have been made on behalf of a program. The claimed benefits to be achieved by a program are, in effect, program goals. Educators who plan to monitor, assess, and report the progress and outcomes of qualitative art instruction will want to review, evaluate, and explicitly state the purposes of visual art education at both elementary and secondary levels, as agreed upon by all parties—school boards, administrators and building principals, art teachers and art supervisors. A statement of purpose should guide all aspects of program implementation, including the provision of adequate instructional time, facilities, audiovisual and print media, and art-working materials.

The first chapter of this monograph stated that the primary purpose and value of "qualitative" art education is the empowerment of all students with competencies and attitudes for perceiving, interpreting, appreciating, and re-presenting in art media the humanistic contents of visual art objects from many world cultures. These humanistic contents constitute what writers of the National

67

Endowment for the Arts report, *Toward Civilization* (43), term "the artistic heritage that is ours." In addition, a prime goal of qualitative art education is to develop and enhance student aptitudes and attitudes for making original objects that may contribute to the "continuing evolution" of the "heritage that is ours"(43).

In sum, the purpose of qualitative visual art education is the development and enhancement in all students of motivation and competency for gaining cultural meanings and for contributing to the ongoing growth of human culture through the perception and production of nonverbally expressive visual art objects.

ASSESSING PROGRAM EFFECTIVENESS

"Program-effectiveness evaluation" means objective appraisal of the degree to which all the resources and methods that constitute an educational program are contributing to the stated program purposes that justify its existence. In the case of qualitative art education, such appraisal is reality-based (i.e., fact-based, evidentially grounded) judgment of the degree to which students who have experienced the program for considerable periods of time are progressively improving their competencies for *appreciative interpretation and production* of culturally significant visual art objects.

Fundamental Competencies of Qualitative Art

In Chapter 1 the fundamental (i.e., the necessary and sufficient) competencies of the visual arts were generalized as follows: (1) *perception* and re-presentation in art media of the primary gestalt patterns that express art-object meanings; (2) *assimilation* of art-object perceptions in personal memory stores; (3) *accommodation* of personal assimilations to new, problematic encounters (e.g., art "problems" posed by art teachers); (4) *association* of human feelings and values with art-object perceptions, assimilations, and accommodations; and (5) *application* of art-object perceptions, assimilations, accommodations, and associations to original student productions in varieties of art media that might contribute to the ongoing evolution of human culture.

The hierarchical order of these competencies is evident. All art abilities grow organically upon the basis of the prime abilities of

68

gestalt perception and the articulation of those gestalts in sensory media. The fundamental gestalt patterns are then assimilated into the perceiver's individually distinctive memory store of personally significant imagery. The assimilated forms constitute Broudy's "allusionary base" for accommodating new, problematic experiences (e.g., for finding visual art solutions to teacher-given "art problems"). Through empathetic projection or affinity, the competent art student—like any mature artist—associates human attitudes, emotions, and values with assimilated and accommodated perceptual gestalts. Finally, the art student and the mature artist are able to form original works in two- and three-dimensional tangible, sensory media that may contribute meaning and value to human society as well as to the individual.

The hierarchical order of generalized art competencies may be set forth on a chart for rating individual student progress toward the goals of qualitative visual art education. Figure 2 is an example of such a chart. It is most useful *not* for individual student grading, as in report cards that "rank" students, but for assessing overall program effectiveness.

At intervals, expert artists and art teachers may randomly select and then evaluate the contents of student "portfolios." These folders or envelopes of student work samples represent the progressive unfolding of the art educational program. When, in accordance with the criteria outlined on the rating chart, the "experts" determine that a majority of sampled students progress toward the high side of rating scales on most performance criteria, it may be credibly stated that the art program is successful.

DEMONSTRATION OF PROGRAM-EFFECTIVENESS EVALUATION

The following pages illustrate how art teachers and supervisor in one school district assessed the effectiveness of their qualitative visual art program.

After adopting a "qualitative" conception of visual art education, all the art teachers and the art supervisor of a school district decided to assess the effectiveness of their approach for "progressively enhancing student competencies for appreciative interpretation and creative

Figure 2
Art Performance Rating Chart

Student _____ School _____

Grade level _____ Time span _____
                            (From)   (To)

Explanation: The art educator checks one box of each line to show his/her rating of a student's performance of the ability described on each line. If the student has not demonstrated the ability, the educator checks the box of the first column, under 0. Other ratings range from 1, "little," to 4, "superior."

Portfolio work samples and performances during art classtime demonstrate student attainment of the following levels of ability:

	Rating Scale				
I. *Perception*.The student—	0	1	2	3	4
1. Detects and depicts an object's major gestalt form.					
2. Depicts the expressive dynamics of the object(s).					
3. Depicts minor elements that echo the major form(s)					
4. Depicts synesthetic qualities (e.g., weight, texture).					
5. Interprets with metaphoric, figurative language.					
II. *Assimilation*. The student—					
6. Depicts personal associations (with I. Perception).					
7. Depicts analogous/metaphoric memory imagery.					
8. Explains associations with figurative language.					
III. *Accommodation*. The student—					
9. Shows openness to new unusual tasks, ideas, problems.					
10. Sketches possible connections between III.9 and I and II.					
11. Explains connections with figurative language.					
12. Transforms best sketch-idea into an art composition.					
13. Improvises with art-composition media.					
14. Incorporates elements of I and II.					
15. Integrates all elements in a unified composition.					
IV. *Association*. The student—					
16. Depicts expressive (e.g., "sad," "stern") forms.					
17. Depicts synesthetic (e.g., "blatant ") forms.					
18. Evaluates with metaphoric language (e.g., "pompous").					
V. *Application*. The student—					
19. Transforms experiences of I–IV into original art.					
20. Integrates elements of I–IV in unified compositions.					

production of culturally significant art objects" during one school year with a representative sample of middle-school students.

The art educators decided to evaluate the progress of approximately 80 seventh graders toward the competencies listed on the teacher-designed Art Performance Rating Chart (Figure 2). The students were divided among three randomly selected class groups of one of the district's three middle schools. Each group had been scheduled, by the building principal, to receive 100 minutes of art instruction weekly.

The art specialist assigned to the three student groups agreed to implement contents and methods of instruction that were in harmony with a "qualitative" conception. To clarify the conception, all the district art teachers and their supervisor engaged in brainstorming. Through this process, they developed a checklist of what they considered to be "ideal conditions" for developing and enhancing art abilities of *perception, assimilation, accommodation, association*, and *application*.

Using evaluative scales from "none" and 'little" to "much" and "excellent," the educators titled their checklist Art Educational Conditions (see Figure 3). They asked the district art supervisor to regularly visit and rate the sample classes for degree of agreement with their list of qualitative educational conditions. The supervisor's visits and ratings constituted *formative evaluation*. Given supervisory reports of "none," "little," or "some" on some criteria, the teachers planned and designed new educational resources and methods that the pilot teacher implemented to improve the qualitativeness of the program.

Preassessment Activities. To determine the ability levels of the seventh graders at the beginning of the experimental program-implementation year, the district art teachers and their supervisor prepared some introductory assessment methods and an evaluative instrument.

Their evaluative instrument was a variant of the "semantic differential" described by Osgood and others in *The Measurement of Meaning* (45). It was called Art Expression Scale (see Figure 4). This instrument consisted of 30 opposing adjectives representing categories of metaphoric, synesthetic, and empathetic meaning. Given an art object or reproduction to interpret qualitatively, a student was expected to be able to judge its degree of weightiness or buoyancy, sadness or cheerfulness, warmth or coolness, stillness or liveliness, etc., on a scale from "slightly" to "very."

It was hypothesized that, during the course of the program-implementation year, a majority of students would improve the subtlety of their metaphoric, synesthetic, and empathetic judgments when presented specific art reproductions. To set viable standards for subtlety, each of the district's 14 elementary and secondary art teachers used the scale for each of the 30 opposing adjectives (Figure 4) to respond to the six preassessment art reproductions that were to be presented to students. The teacher responses were averaged and the medians were considered to be good objectives for the development of subtle perceptual and interpretive art abilities in students.

Figure 3
Art Educational Conditions

Classroom _____ Student group_____ Grade(s)_____

School _____ Date of observation _____ Time span _____

Explanation: The art program evaluator checks one box on each line that describes a condition that is conducive to student achievement of qualitative art abilities. When the evaluator observes that a condition is not present during instruction, he/she checks the box in the column under 0. Other ratings range from 1, "little," to 4, "excellent."

Observed conditions for student achievement were—

Rating Scale

	0	1	2	3	4
I. For developing *Perception*—					
1. Provision of exemplary cultural art objects					
2. Perceptual access to exemplary art objects					
3. Attention focused on major gestalt forms					
4. Attention focused on expressive dynamics					
5. Art media available for showing perceptions					
6. Instruction provided in art media skills					
7. Interpretive language elicited/facilitated					
II. For facilitating *assimilation*—					
8. Recall of relevant memories stimulated					
9. Metaphoric/figurative reflection induced					
10. Metaphoric/figurative depiction facilitated					
11. Metaphoric/figurative language induced					
III. For inducing/guiding *accommodation*—					
12. Problems given to challenge imagination					
13. Problems related to prior experiences (I and II)					
14. Students guided to sketch possible solutions					
15. Students induced to think figuratively					
16. Students helped to evaluate their sketches					
17. Students helped to select best solutions					
18. Students induced to improvise with media					
19. Media-skills instruction given as needed					
20. Composition/design concepts taught as needed					
IV. For inducing *association* and *evaluation*—					
21. Students helped to associate forms and feelings					
22. Form-feeling empathetic language elicited					
23. Intersensory perception/expression elicited					
24. Metaphoric evaluative language elicited					
V. For facilitating *application* of artistic learning—					
25. Students challenged, helped, and guided to integrate learnings I through IV into original artworks.					

Figure 4
Art Expression Scale

Student _____ School _____ Grade ____

Date _____ Art Item Studied _____

Directions: Check *one* box on each line that best expresses your response to the art item you are viewing. If words at either end of a line do not relate to the artwork, check the NEITHER box.

This artwork seems—

1. Neither   3. Quite
2. Slightly   4. Very

	4	3	2	1	2	3	4		
1. Weighty								Light/Buoyant	1.
2. Serious/Sad								Cheerful	2.
3. Calm/Restful								Excited	3.
4. Quiet								Loud	4.
5. Smooth								Rough	5.
6. Cool								Warm	6.
7. Tender								Harsh	7.
8. Enclosed								Spacious	8.
9. Restrained								Expansive	9.
10. Passive								Aggressive	10.
11. Burdened								Relieved	11.
12. Relaxed								Nervous	12.
13. Unified								Broken/Jumbled	13.
14. Serene								Disturbed	14.
15. Angular								Curving	15.
16. Yielding								Striving	16.
17. Modest/Humble								Bold/Proud	17.
18. Fearful								Confident	18.
19. Sober/Stern								Amusing/Comical	19.
20. Kind								Cruel	20.
21. Distant								Close up	21.
22. Still								Lively	22.
23. Friendly								Threatening	23.
24. Graceful								Awkward	24.
25. Soft								Hard	25.
26. Dark								Bright	26.
27. Gradual								Abrupt	27.
28. Plain/Simple								Fancy/Complex	28.
29. Rigid/Regulated								Free-flowing	29.
30. Sturdy								Fragile	30.

Preassessment Items. The items selected by the district's art teachers to assess the perceptual and interpretive abilities of the seventh graders were (1) Picasso's *Girl Before a Mirror* (1932); (2) van Gogh's *Night Cafe at Arles* (1888); (3) Boccioni's *Forms of Continuity in Space* (1913); (4) a set of late nineteenth century masks from Gabon and the Ivory Coast of Africa (cf. Leuzinger [39, P. 158, 101]); (5) Fragonard's *Blindman's Buff* (1770s); and (6) van Gogh's *Irises* (ca. 1889).

An analysis of art teachers' responses on the Art Expression Scale shows that they found van Gogh's *Night Cafe* "very" (i.e., value +4) warm, harsh, nervous, disturbed, threatening, bright, and abrupt; and "quite" (i.e., value +3) sad, enclosed, restrained, burdened, angular, fearful, stern, awkward, and hard. In comparison, during the first week of their seventh-grade school year, analysis showed that a majority of the experimental subjects assigned a value of +4 ("very") to sad, nervous, disturbed, and fearful, and a value of +3 ("quite") to calm, quiet, warm, burdened, stern, still, awkward, plain/simple. In general, the student preassessment responses were *literal* rather than *metaphoric* (e.g., they literally described the *Night Cafe* scene with "calm," "quiet," "plain/simple," and the late-night cafe patrons with word choices of "sad," "nervous," "disturbed," "fearful," and "burdened") as compared with the more figurative, synesthetic, and subtly empathetic word choices of the teachers. It was assumed, rightly as it later turned out, that, as the year progressed, the seventh graders would more nearly approach professional art-teacher selections of metaphoric and empathetic words that subtly interpret visual art gestalt qualities.

Preassessment Lesson. Immediately following this preassessment activity, students were engaged in an instructional sequence designed (by the 14 district art teachers) to pretest their abilities of *assimilation, accommodation and association* (cf. Figure 2, items II through IV). The sequence was conducted by the voluntary pilot art teacher with guidance from the elementary and secondary art teachers. The instructional method and the quality of student participation were critically observed by the art supervisor. The entire sequence occurred within 200 minutes, or four 50-minute art periods.

Initially, students were asked to select one of the six cultural art items that they had responded to on the Art Expression Scale. Each student reviewed and wrote all the "very" (value +4) and "quite" (value +3) words that she/he had assigned to the selected art item. Each student also was asked to reflect upon a personal experience that was "like" both the subject-matter and the "very" and "quite" expression-words he or she had assigned to the item. Group brainstorming activities, led and recorded on an easel pad by the pilot art teacher, helped stimulate student recall and expressive interpretation of personal memory experiences relevant to the preassessment art items. Recollections and interpretations were sketched in both graphic and verbal media by each student.

Accommodation Activities. Students were stimulated to imagine a pre-sent-day or possible future cultural situation that might be artistically ex-pressed in ways similar to the "very" and "quite" qualities each had recorded in words and sketches related to one of the six preassess-ment art items. Students imagined, sketched, and briefly verbalized such "connections" as a prisoner torture and interrogation room (they had been told of Vincent's letter to Theo: "In my picture of the 'Night-Cafe' I tried to express the idea that the cafe is a place where one can ruin oneself, go mad, or commit a crime."); a jet-propelled, Buck Rog-ers'-type space traveler for Boccioni's bronze sculpture; Halloween masks and scarecrow figures for the African spirit masks; and a Mardi Gras masquerade party for Fragonard's elegant rococo-style painting.

Improvising with a rich variety of materials, each student composed a two-dimensional collage or a three-dimensional assemblage to repre-sent an art idea that had come to mind from reflecting upon the ex-pressive qualities of one of the six preassessment items. Through indi-viudalized instruction, the pilot teacher helped students emphasize abstract expressive qualities (e.g., "swirling shapes" or "intense hot colors") rather than the literal, factual qualities of the preassessment art items that they were imaginatively recreating. The teacher also helped students unify their collages or assemblages.

Association Activities. To generate metaphoric, synesthetic, empathet-ic, and evaluative thinking, the pilot art teacher asked each seventh grader to select *another student's* collage or assemblage and to rate its sensory-expressive qualities, using the art expression scale (see Fig-ure 4). To facilitate this process, the teacher provided dictionaries and asked students to write synonyms and explanations for the meanings of unfamiliar words found on the scale.

Finally, the teacher asked each student to identify another student's original art-reference item (i.e., one of the six preassessment art repro-ductions) and *to evaluate the artistic relevance* of the student-made collage or assemblage to the reproduction. "Relevance" was defined as sense-perceptual similarity (e.g., "color warmth," "symmetrical bal-ance," "free-flowing, curvy design," "rigid, geometric shape," or "ex-pansive spaciousness") and expressive concordance (e.g., "cheerful-ness," "nervousness," "boldness," or "serenity") between the student collage or assemblage and the preassessment item.

Student Performance Rating. Using the Art Performance Rating Chart (Figure 2), the district art teachers evaluated each student's qual-itative art performances. Ratings were based upon evidence provided by work-samples that were dated and stored in student portfolios. This evidence of qualitative aptitude was amplified by anecdotal records and recollections of student performance provided by both the pilot teacher and the art supervisor who had observed all preassessment activities.

Postassessment Activities. For two weeks near the end of the school year, the pilot art teacher recapitulated all the preassessment activities, including student ratings of the metaphoric, synesthetic, and empathetic qualities of Picasso's *Girl Before a Mirror*, van Gogh's *Night Cafe* and *Irises*, Boccioni's *Forms of Continuity*, the two late-nineteenth-century African masks, and Fragonard's *Blindman's Buff*.

Immediately preceding this recapitulation, all the district art teachers and the supervisor again responded to the six preassessment art items by rating their qualities on the Art Expression Scale. These responses differed somewhat from their earlier ones. As a result of this participation in the pilot implementation process, the teachers and the art supervisor had evidently refined their abilities of qualitative perception and interpretation. Pre- and post-teacher-response averages for each of the 30 adjectives were calculated. For purposes of *program-effectiveness evaluation*, these averages were considered to be appropriate standards for judging student progress toward the perceptual and interpretive ability objectives of the experimental program.

Though the postassessment lesson paralleled that of the first part of the school year, each of the 80 seventh graders worked from an art reproduction different from the one he/she had previously selected. Students were encouraged and guided to imagine and produce new expressions of assimilation, accommodation, and association. Each student also was given the time, resources, and instructional assistance needed to produce an original artwork that incorporated and synthesized ideas and abilities that had been initiated and refined during the perception, assimilation, accommodation, and association phases of the postassessment exercise. Thus, each student's year culminated with an art production experience designed to demonstrate qualitative application abilities (category V of Figure 2.)

Summative Assessment. The district art teachers averaged all art expression scale ratings that the seventh graders had marked for the six art reproduction items both at the beginning and the end of the year. These averages demonstrated that (a) student ratings of the metaphoric, synesthetic, and empathetic qualities of the six pre- and postassessment art items changed significantly during the year, and (b) the change was toward the ratings produced by the district art teachers and their supervisor. Thus, it was appropriate to report to all constituencies—the local board of education, district and building administrators, all other teachers of the district, students and their parents—that the perceptual and interpretive art abilities of students progressed in the direction of the abilities of professional artist-teachers during one pilot-implementation year of "qualitative visual art education."

Comparison of district art teacher ratings of the preassessment and postassessment art activity performances of the 80 experimental subjects demonstrated that a majority of students advanced from "little" to "excellent" on all *perception, assimilation,* and *association* items of

76

Figure 2. A majority of the seventh graders advanced from "none" and "little" to "much" on the *accommodation* and *application* abilities listed on the rating chart. *All* students demonstrated some degree of growth on at least 15 of the 20 art-ability items listed. These facts were reported to the various constituencies of the school district.

Benefits of Program-Effectiveness Evaluation

The art educators who voluntarily participated in the assessment process described above gained several important professional benefits. Perhaps they benefited most from their experiences of collegial communication and teamwork. They enjoyed the pleasures of comparing and contrasting individual dispositions and styles and then of brainstorming common ground for merging these differences and similarities into a unitary conception that they termed "qualitative art education." Having clarified their mutual conception in terms of concretely observable and—to a degree—measurable teacher and student behaviors, these professional colleagues imagined and then implemented a process for determining how their conceptualized "qualitative" methodology would in fact help all students develop desirable art abilities. Through these collegial activities, the districtwide team of art educators demonstrated that they are an autonomous group that can conceptualize and agree upon common purposes and methodologies and can then effectively activate and focus teacher abilities and instructional resources on behalf of the agreed-upon conceptions.

In addition to collegiality and professional autonomy, the educators who shared in this definition and evaluation process gained much credibility for the practice of art education in their community. Though evaluation was limited to monitoring and assessing art progress for only three regularly scheduled and average-sized class groups at one middle school, the various constituencies of the school district as a whole could accept the demonstration of gains by about 80 seventh graders as representing the beneficial effect of qualitative art education at all grade levels. These groups were then willing to argue for continuing financial support of qualitative art educational practice throughout the school district.

77

BIBLIOGRAPHY

1. Arnheim, R. *Picasso's Guernica, the Genesis of a Painting*. Berkeley: University of California Press, 1962.
2. _____. *Art and Visual Perception: A Psychology of the Creative Eye.* (New version.) Berkeley: University of California Press, 1974.
3. Bennett, W. J. "Why the Arts are Essential." *Educational Leadership* 45, no. 4 (1987–1988): 4–5.
4. Bloom, B.S.; Hastings, J. Thomas; and Madaus, G.F. *Handbook on Formative and Summative Evaluation of Student Learning*. New York: McGraw-Hill Book Co., 1971.
5. Boyer, E. L. *High School: A Report on Secondary Education in America*. New York: Harper and Row, 1983.
6. _____. "Art as Language: Its Place in the Schools." In *Beyond Creating: The Place for Art in America's Schools,* edited by Getty Center for Education in the Arts, pp. 8–9. Los Angeles: J. Paul Getty Trust, 1985.
7. Brigham, D. L. "Dewey's Concept of Qualitative Thought as a Basis for the Teaching of Art." *Dissertation Abstracts International* 46 (1985): 53A. University Microfilms DA 85–04276.
7a. Brigham, D. L. "Dewey's Qualitative Thought as Exemplary Art Education." *Art Education* 42, no. 2 (March 1989): 14–22.
8. Broudy H.S. "Arts Education: Necessary or Just Nice?" *Phi Delta Kappan* (1979): 347–50.
9. _____. *The Role of Imagery in Learning*. Los Angeles: Getty Center for Education in the Arts, 1987.
10. Brown, J. C. "Art Education Flunks Out." *Art News* 87, no.1 (1988): 190.
11. Bruner, J. S. *Toward a Theory of Instruction*. New York: W. W. Norton, 1966.
12. Chapman, L. H. *Discover Art, Teacher's Edition, Grade 4.* Worcester, Mass.: Davis Publications, 1985.
13. Clark, G. A.; Day, M. D.; and Greer, W. D. "Discipline-Based Art Education: Becoming Students of Art." *Journal of Aesthetic Education* 21, no. 2 (1987): 129–93.
14. Dewey, J. "My Pedagogic Creed." In *The Teacher and the Taught,* edited by R. Gross, pp. 148–49. Dell Publishing Co., 1963.
15. _____. "Qualitative Thought." In *Philosophy and Civilization,* edited by J. Dewey, pp. 93–116. Gloucester, Mass.: Peter Smith Publisher, 1968. (Original work published in 1931)
16. _____. *Art as Experience*. New York: G. P. Putnam's Sons, Perigee Books, 1980. (Original work published in 1934)
17. Eisner, E. W. *Educating Artistic Vision*. New York: Macmillan, 1972.

18. ———. "What Do Children Learn When They Paint?" *Art Education* 31, no. 3 (1978): 7.

19. ———. "Reading and the Creation of Meaning." In *Reading, the Arts, and the Creation of Meaning,* edited by E. W. Eisner. Reston, Va.: National Art Education Association, 1978.

20. ———. "The Arts as a Way of Knowing." *Principal* 60, no. 1 (1980): 11–14.

21. ———. "Can the Humanities Be Taught in American Public Schools?" In *The Humanities in Precollegiate Education,* edited by B. Ladner, pp. 112–29. 83d Yearbook of the National Society for the Study of Education. Chicago: the Society, 1984.

22. ———. "Why Art in Education and Why Art Education." In *Beyond Creating: The Place for Art in America's Schools* edited by Getty Center for Education in the Arts, pp. 64–69. Los Angeles: J. Paul Getty Trust, 1985.

23. ———. *The Role of Discipline-Based Art Education in America's Schools.* Los Angeles: Getty Center for Education in the Arts, 1986.

24. ———. "Structure and Magic in Discipline-Based Art Eduction." In Proceedings of a National Invitational Conference, *Discipline-Based Art Education: What Forms Will It Take?* Los Angeles: Getty Center for Education in the Arts, 1987.

25. Feinstein, H. "Art as Visual Metaphor." *Art Education* 38, no. 4, (1985): 26–29.

26. Feldman, E. B. "Art in the Mainstream: Ideology and Hope. *Art Education* 36, no. 4, (1983): 9.

27. Gardner, H. "Conversation with Howard Gardner by Ron Brandt." *Educational Leadership* (December 1987–January 1988): 31–34.

28. Geffroy, G. Cited in *Impressionism,* edited by *Réalités,* pp. 134–41, 254–55. Secaucus, N.J.: Chartwell Books, 1976. Originally published in French as *L'Impressionisme,* 1971.

29. Getty Center for Education in the Arts, ed. *Beyond Creating: The Place for Art in America's Schools.* Los Angeles: J. Paul Getty Trust, 1985.

30. Goodlad, J. I. *A Place Called School: Prospects for the Future.* New York: McGraw-Hill, 1983.

31. Goodrich, L., and Bry, D. *Georgia O'Keeffe.* New York: Whitney Museum of American Art, 1970. (Distributed by Praeger)

32. Greene, M. "Excellence and the Basics." In *The Fourth 'R': Risk,* edited by C. Eisele, pp. 22—28. Normal, Ill.: John Dewey Society for the Study of Education and Culture, 1984.

33. ———. "The Art of Being Present: Educating for Aesthetic Encounters." *Boston University Journal of Education* 166 (1984): 123—35.

34. Hodsoll, F.S.M. "Arts and the N.E.A." *Design for Arts in Education* 85, no. 2 (1983): 5.

35. ———. Keynote Address to a National Invitational Conference on Art Education. In *Discipline-Based Art Education: What Forms Will It Take?*

edited by Getty Center for Education in the Arts, pp. 102–3, 104–13, 109. Los Angeles: J. Paul Getty Trust, 1987.

36. Kepes, G. *The New Landscape in Art and Science.* Chicago: Paul Theobald and Co., 1956.

37. Langer, S. K. *Feeling and Form: A Theory of Art.* New York: Charles Scribner's Sons, 1953.

38. _____. *Mind: An Essay on Human Feeling.* Baltimore: Johns Hopkins Press, 1967.

39. Leuzinger, E. *The Art of Africa.* New York: Crown, 1960.

40. Lipman, S. "Cultural Policy: Whither America, Whither Government?" *New Criterion* 3 (1984): 14.

41. Moore, H. "Notes on Sculpture." In *The Creative Process: A Symposium,* edited by B. Ghiselin, pp. 73—78. New York: New American Library, Mentor Books, 1952.

42. National Commission on Excellence in Education. *A Nation At Risk: The Imperative for Educational Reform.* Washington, D.C.: U.S. Government Printing Office, 1983.

43. National Endowment for the Arts. Overview, *Toward Civilization. NAEA News* 30, no. 3 (1988): 3–7.

44. O'Keeffe, G. Exhibition catalog, *An American Place* Gallery, New York, 1944. Cited in *Georgia O'Keeffe,* edited by G. O'Keeffe, Plate 74. New York: Viking Press, 1976.

45. Osgood, C. E.; Suci, G. J.; and Tannenbaum, P., eds. *The Measurement of Meaning.* Urbana, Ill.: University of Illinois Press, 1957.

46. Penguin Books. *Georgia O'Keeffe.* New York: Penguin Books, 1977. (First published by Viking Press, 1976)

47. Randall, J. R., Jr. "Qualities, Qualification, and the Aesthetic Transaction." In *Nature and Historical Experience,* edited by J. R. Randall, Jr. New York: Columbia University Press, 1958.

48. Read, H. *Icon and Idea.* New York: Schocken Books, 1965.

49. Réalités, eds. *Impressionism.* Secaucus, N.J.: Chartwell Books, 1976.

50. Rico G. L. "Reading for Non-literal Meaning." In *Reading, the Arts, and the Creation of Meaning,* edited by E. W. Eisner. Reston, Va.: National Art Education Association, 1978.

51. Roters, E. *Painters of the Bauhaus.* New York: F. A. Praeger, 1965.

52. Rubin, W. *Pablo Picasso, A Restrospective.* New York: Museum of Modern Art, 1980.

53. Schneider, P. *The World of Watteau.* New York: Time, 1967.

54. Selz, J. *Edvard Munch.* New York: Crown Publishers, 1974.

55. Smith, R. A. "Policy for Arts Education; Whither the Schools, Whither the Public and Private Sectors?" *Design for Arts in Education* 89, no. 4 (March/April 1988): 2–11.

56. Thoreau, H. D. *Walden.* New York: W. W. Norton, 1951.

57. Wright, C. *French Painting.* New York: Mayflower Books, 1979.